THE DOG LIFE COACH

Lessons in Love and Life

Alison Hatton

The Dog Life Coach
Lessons in Love and Life

thedoglifecoach@animalhealingtherapies.co.uk

ISBN: 9798852708540

Book cover design by 100 Covers

Published by Alison Hatton

Printed by Amazon KDP Print

www.animalhealingtherapies.co.uk/the-dog-life-coach

CONTENTS

INTRODUCTION

Have you ever wondered what life lessons dogs could teach us and how we might go about discovering them? Well, that's exactly what this book is here to show you. Imagine it as a unique blend of a personal counsellor, life coach and compass all bundled together. Its purpose? To explore the deep emotional wisdom that dogs are so willing to share with us. We can draw inspiration from their incredible emotional depth and use this wisdom as tools to help us navigate the highs and lows of life together.

I've always had dogs in my life, right from when I was a child. Their unwavering love and loyalty were constant companions, sticking by me through thick and thin. Our family dogs, Tiny and Toby, were perfect examples of what unconditional love looked like. There have been tough times in my life when I've wrestled with self-doubt and a sense of lost direction. In these moments I've often questioned, 'How can I create a life that mirrors who I am?' and 'Why am I burdened with anxiety and feelings of not being good enough?'

These questions sparked a journey towards healing, self-growth and understanding. Yet, despite countless books, courses and other resources I found the guidance I sought was lacking usefulness and clarity, and I often found myself grasping at straws, struggling to find clear, helpful guidance. It turns out the answers I sought were right under my nose, in my interactions with my dogs and in observing my friends' relationships with their dogs and I'll be sharing some of those stories with you throughout this book. Their simple yet profound wisdom shaped my path to self-belief, acceptance and happiness. Inspired by this success, I put pen to paper, and voila, this book was born.

The insights from this book aren't only restricted to these pages; they're also shared through my online courses. Why do people find it so helpful? Because it's relatable. We can see these traits in dogs, and by choosing to mirror how they engage with the world and the people in it we can learn to be 'more dog'. This involves expressing qualities like unconditional love, self-compassion, resilience and forgiveness, to mention a few. It's all about embracing the beautiful qualities dogs display so naturally.

In a dog's world love is unconditional, moments are lived to the fullest and forgiveness comes easily. But this isn't just a book about dogs; it's about learning to live like a dog unconditionally, relentlessly and forgivingly. It's not only about appreciating dogs; it's about learning from them, their unwavering love, art of living in the present and their capacity to find joy in the simple things in life.

This book takes you on a journey that explores their emotionally vibrant world, and it's through this shared journey that you come to realise the lessons dogs can teach you. Looking through their eyes you'll uncover universal truths about empathy, self-care, gratitude and more. This isn't simply a shared journey; it's a roadmap to understanding and practicing the profound life lessons that dogs offer, creating a path towards a self-compassionate and fulfilling life.

To begin our journey, let's take a step back into the mists of time, when every day was a battle for survival, for that's where the story of humans and dogs begins. Wolves, the great-grandfather of dogs, saw the perks of hanging out with us - food scraps, a bit of warmth, a sense of safety, pretty simple stuff - but back then, it was a big deal. And it wasn't a one-way street. We saw the benefits too. They served as lookouts for danger and eventually became loyal friends. This friendship wasn't an overnight thing.

It took thousands of years of give and take, understanding and cooperation, leading to the amazing animals we call dogs today. Communication wasn't based on words or grammar but on something much more raw and real. It came from shared emotions and needs, allowing us to grow closer. Dogs learnt to read our gestures, faces and even the tone of our voice and we got the hang of their barks, growls and tail-wagging antics.

Fast forward to today, and this bond has blossomed into something truly extraordinary. The connection we share with dogs is magical. It's based on empathy, mutual respect and often surpasses many relationships we share with other humans. Dogs give without keeping score, love without judging and forgive without a second thought. They have this amazing ability to understand our moods and respond in exactly the right way, offering comfort when we're sad and keeping us company when we're feeling lonely. They display virtues like patience, loyalty and the joy of living in the moment, things that we humans can often struggle with. They're like our personal life coach, showing us the way towards better self-care, how to show more empathy, self-compassion, forgiveness and how to love unconditionally. They teach us how to navigate life's maze with grace and courage and they can guide us towards overall healthier emotional lives.

As we dive into the chapters of this book, we're going to be uncovering the many traits that make dogs such amazing teachers and friends. Each chapter focuses on a different quality that our dogs show so beautifully: their boundless love, unwavering loyalty, knack for living in the moment and more. We'll not only explore these qualities but we will also learn how we can embody and express them in our own lives. Each chapter comes with practical exercises and I would encourage you to carry these out; they are included to enhance your understanding. As you engage with these exercises, you'll integrate the wisdom of dogs and subtly change the way you see and interact with the world. This book isn't just about reading; it's about living. Each chapter, each exercise, is a step closer to embracing a way of life that's defined by compassion, forgiveness, love and mindfulness.

As we journey together through this book, I hope that you'll not only learn about the wisdom dogs offer but also live it, make it a part of you and let it enrich your life. Are you ready to embark on this journey, a journey that could redefine the way you live and love?

* * *

CHAPTER 1: UNCONDITIONAL LOVE

Throughout my childhood pets were always a part of our home. Tiny, the Jack Russell, tan and white, confident and yappy. Toby, a timid little black mongrel, slightly deaf with age, sporting a greying muzzle. Tiny was in charge; Toby just followed the rules. No one is sure how he managed it, but Toby became the proud father of two adorable puppies. Jenny was his carbon copy, pure black, tiny and delicate. Roly was twice the size and made sure you knew of his need for constant attention and love, Tiny mark two. I begged to keep them but knew this was not practical and instead we made sure we found them good homes.

I think Roly got the better deal. He was going home with a family who had his basket ready, filled with hand-crocheted blankets that fitted nicely next to their real fireplace.

'We have bought an extra box of Weetabix. Our old dog loved one for his mid-morning snack with a drop of warm milk.'

I'm sure at that moment Roly understood perfectly what was being discussed, and his contented little sigh said it all.

As a child things were difficult. Home was often a tense battleground. Weapons were words with heated arguments between my parents lasting late into the night. I pushed my fingers into my ears, desperate to drown out the noise, holding my breath, fearing the worst. As I lay in bed, a cold wet nose would often push my bedroom door ajar and I would hear the soft pad of paws cross the carpet towards me. It was Toby. He would sense my need for him to be near as he had done many nights before. I would lift the covers, and he would find that spot in the crook of my arm, waiting for him to fill. As I listened to the steady beat of his heart next to mine I gently stroked his ears and gave silent thanks for our pets' ability to heal us.

I was blessed with having Toby in my life for many years, and his unwavering love was constant. Imagine the endless and steadfast love that a dog has for its human. You may have been lucky enough to have experienced this yourself. No matter what sort of day you've had your dog is always there, tail wagging and full of love. This is unconditional love at its purest, loving with no limits or conditions, and it's not just a characteristic of our dogs but a lesson they're teaching us.

Have you ever stopped and thought about how dogs really see us? They don't care about how big our bank balance is or what job title we've earned. The mistakes we've made, the big wins we've had, the heartbreaks we've survived. To them, they're just background noise. To dogs, we are their whole universe and are loved just as we are. It's a love that comes without terms and conditions. There is no fine print to read. It's there, limitless and always present. Isn't that a lesson in love worth taking to heart?

Have you ever given a thought to how a dog expresses their love for you? You know, the enthusiastic tail wagging that greets you at the door, the comforting snuggle when you're down, that protective growl when they sense danger lurking. It's like their entire existence orbits around this selfless simple act of loving you. Now, imagine for a second, what if we, as humans, infused that same pure spirit into our relationships? Could we possibly love ourselves and each other without judgement or conditions? How do you think that might transform our emotional wellbeing, our interactions with each other and even our perspective of the world?

Loving unconditionally as dogs do is no easy feat. It requires patience, perseverance and a good amount of introspection. As humans we're a wonderfully complex mix of emotions, thought processes and behaviours. Sometimes this complexity can cloud our approach to love. Without even realising it we might attach conditions to our love. We might find ourselves making judgements, forming expectations and even withdrawing love when we feel wronged. It's as if we're playing a tug of war with our emotions, which can be exhausting.

Take a moment to think about your own experiences. Have there been times when you've felt that your love came with conditions? Maybe you've thought, *I'll show them more affection when they treat me better,* or *They don't deserve my love if they don't appreciate it.* These are not unusual thoughts and you're not alone if you've had them. It's part of our human instinct to protect ourselves from being hurt or taken for granted.

But then we look at our dogs and it's a whole different world. Dogs are like these beautiful, selfless beings that radiate love and positivity. Their love isn't dictated by moods or grievances. It's consistent, free and enriching. It's this kind of love that we can learn to replicate. It may not happen overnight, but with conscious effort and self-awareness, we can strive to love more like our dogs do. We can work to shed our judgements, curb our expectations and be more forgiving. We can aim to make our love less about 'getting' and more about 'giving'. It's a journey, but a rewarding one, wouldn't you agree? As we embrace this kind of love, we're not only improving our relationships but also nourishing our own well-being.

Unconditional love starts from within, and self-love is the foundation of this journey. It's like preparing to plant a garden and the first step is to nourish the soil. In the same way we need to nurture our inner selves first before we can fully love others unconditionally. Self-love isn't about being selfish or self-centred, far from it. It's about accepting ourselves, flaws and all. It's about celebrating the person we are and recognising the person we can become.

Self-love is like turning on a light within ourselves, illuminating our true essence and acknowledging that we're a blend of many things: our passions, flaws and our strengths. Each one of us has a unique spark that drives us, a passion that sets our soul on fire. This might be creativity, empathy, determination or a multitude of other things. You might wonder how this translates into unconditional love for others? When we accept and love ourselves we can extend the same compassion and acceptance to others. We become less judgemental, more understanding and more patient. We learn to love others not for what they can do for us but simply for who they are.

The idea of self-love often gets mistaken for narcissism or being self-centred, but it's actually the furthest thing from that. Let's look at it this way, self-love is like building your own house. You need a solid foundation and that's what self-love does for you. It lays a strong base upon which everything else is built. Self-love isn't just about accepting compliments or pampering yourself; it's about really diving deep into your heart, discovering what makes you YOU, and then falling in love with that, one day at a time. It's a journey of self-discovery towards understanding and accepting ourselves with all our quirks, strengths and flaws. It’s a continual process of self-reflection and growth. Bad days happen but that doesn't change your worth. You are good enough. You always were and you always will be.

The beauty of embarking on this path of self-love is that it doesn't just stop at us. It influences our relationships too. When we respect and love ourselves, we set the bar for how we want to be treated by others. We adopt healthier relationships because we're clear about our self-worth and aren't willing to settle for anything less. As we cultivate self-love, we foster resilience and a positive self-image. It's like nurturing a plant. You water it, ensure it gets enough sunlight and slowly you see it begin to grow, becoming stronger and blooming beautifully. That's exactly what self-love does to us. It strengthens us from within, and as a result love, compassion and kindness become a natural extension of who we are.

Think about the times we stumble and make mistakes. Isn't it natural to beat ourselves up a bit, to play the blame game, often pointing the finger at ourselves? But that's where self-love, the self-love dogs show us, steps in. It softly whispers, 'Hey, it's okay to trip up. It's okay to make mistakes. You're human and that's part of the package. Let's pick ourselves up, dust ourselves off and try again'. It's this voice that encourages us to extend the same compassion and patience to ourselves that we would to a best friend who's having a tough time. And the celebrations? That's self-love throwing a party, cheering for us, encouraging us to rejoice in our successes. Each success, each win, is a stepping-stone, building towards a stronger, more resilient self. So, if we make self-love a habit, how transformative would that be for the way we perceive ourselves and others?

When we practice self-love we realise that we are invaluable, not because of our possessions but merely because of our existence, our individuality. And once we truly grasp this concept? That's when the magic happens. We can extend this unconditional love to others, to love them just as dogs do. Unconditional love, what a powerful phrase that is. It's about embodying love the way dogs do - no prejudices and no strings attached, just authentic, unfiltered love. It means setting aside rigid notions and biases and embracing empathy and understanding instead. It's about unlocking our heart and accepting people as they are, not how we wish they were, appreciating their distinctiveness, talents and their vulnerabilities. Every person has their own narrative, strengths and struggles.

Empathy is like taking a walk in someone else's shoes, seeing the world from their perspective. It requires us to step outside of our comfort zone and immerse ourselves in another person's experience. When we empathise we create an environment where acceptance and respect thrive, a space where people can truly be themselves, in all their beauty and imperfections. This empathetic approach allows us to form deeper connections and forge relationships that are not just surface-level but are truly meaningful. We go beyond the surface to discover the real treasure that lies within each individual.

Isn't it fascinating how dogs seem to tune into our feelings? When we're down, they're there, offering comfort. When we're elated they share in our joy. Their empathy seems almost instinctual, doesn't it? And that's the beauty of it. We, too, can strive to boost our empathy, to be more attuned to the emotions and experiences of others. It's like trying to develop our own superpower of understanding and compassion similar to dogs, and this is a significant piece of the puzzle to unconditional love. By fostering empathy we not only understand others better, but we also become more patient, more accepting and more loving. We form bonds that are stronger and more resilient, bonds that can weather life's ups and downs. It's like strengthening the foundations of a house, making it sturdy and secure. Empathy, in this sense, is a bit like relationship cement. It holds everything together, making our connections with others stronger and more meaningful. How beautiful is that?

In the world of unconditional love forgiveness truly is key. It's not just about absolving others, but just as importantly, it's about absolving ourselves too. Let's be honest; we can sometimes be our own worst enemies can't we? We set these incredibly high bars for ourselves and then give ourselves a hard time when we don't quite reach them. But here's a little secret; we're all human, beautifully and brilliantly flawed and that's okay. It's something to be embraced, to be celebrated even.

Now, let's talk about dogs for a moment. Do you ever see them hold on to grudges or dwell on their past mistakes? They're all about the here and now, living each moment as it comes, free from resentment or hard feelings. They teach us to live and love wholeheartedly in the present, without being tethered to the past or too focused on the future. Isn't that a fantastic viewpoint to live by? Imagine if we adopt the same approach, having the ability to forgive and let go. Imagine how liberating it would be, not just in our relationships with others but also in the relationship with ourselves. How would that shift in perspective, that move towards dog-like forgiveness, transform your relationship with others and with yourself?

The ability to let go of negative self-talk, harsh criticisms and unrealistic expectations can come through forgiveness. We can recognise our mistakes as opportunities for growth rather than as reasons for self-punishment, and in doing so, we create a kinder, more compassionate space for ourselves and others. So, the next time you find yourself holding on to a grudge or beating yourself up over a mistake, remember how dogs manage this with their unique ability to forgive and live in the present.

Choosing to love unconditionally, just as dogs do, will take you on a journey filled with joy, peace and a deep sense of satisfaction. It's a choice that not only brings so much richness to our lives but also plays a major part in creating a world filled with more kindness and love. Throughout this book we'll return to this idea of unconditional love. Think of it as our guiding light as we delve into the world of emotional health. As we uncover the wisdom dogs have to teach us, we'll see that unconditional love keeps cropping up as a central theme. It's a testament to just how powerful this kind of love can be in boosting our emotional wellness. So, are ready to explore what it means to love like a dog?

I encourage you to take an active role in the exercises provided throughout this book. Take the time to put into practice the lessons you've learned about cultivating unconditional love.

Reflect on the ways you can extend love and acceptance of yourself and others, free from judgement and conditions. Challenge yourself to let go of grudges and embrace forgiveness, both for others and yourself. Practice empathy and understanding by stepping into the shoes of those around you, which will lead to deeper connections. By actively engaging in these exercises you'll embark on a personal journey of growth, compassion and emotional well-being.

* * *

Exercise 1: Self-Acceptance Journaling

This exercise aims to foster self-acceptance by acknowledging all parts of yourself without judgement. Self-acceptance is the first step towards unconditional self-love. You will need a notebook or journal for this exercise.

Instructions

- Find a calm peaceful place where you won't be disturbed. This may be a quiet room in your house, a favourite spot in a park or anywhere you feel relaxed and peaceful.
- Before you write anything take a moment to set an intention for this exercise. Try saying something like, 'I am here to explore and accept myself, without judgement or expectations.'
- Start by listing your qualities. This can include anything from personality traits to skills and talents. It's important to be comprehensive and to include what you perceive as both positive and negative aspects. For example, 'I am caring, I am a good listener, I procrastinate, I am good at painting, I can be stubborn.'
- As you write each quality, try to not attach judgements or emotions to them. Acknowledge them as they are. They're not good or bad; they're simply parts of you.
- Once you've listed your qualities, go through each one and

consciously accept it as a part of you. You may say something like, 'I accept that I am stubborn' or 'I accept that I am caring.'

- After you've gone through each quality take a moment to reflect on your list. What is it like to accept these aspects of yourself without judgement? Note down any thoughts or feelings that arise.
- Close your journaling session with a moment of gratitude for yourself. Acknowledge the effort you've put into this exercise, and remind yourself of your intention to foster self-acceptance.
- Try to perform this exercise regularly. Set aside some time each day or each week, depending on what suits your schedule.
- Remember, the goal of this exercise is not to change or 'fix' these aspects of yourself but to foster a sense of acceptance towards them. This acceptance is the foundation of unconditional self-love. By acknowledging and accepting all parts of yourself, you're taking significant steps towards loving yourself unconditionally, much like dogs do.

Additional Guidance

- When listing your qualities it's crucial to be honest with yourself. This isn't an exercise in ego-inflation or self-deprecation; it's about getting to know your true self better. Honesty will only enhance the authenticity and effectiveness of this exercise.
- This exercise requires you to suspend any judgment. Don't label your qualities as 'good' or 'bad;' they are simply aspects of you.
- You may come across certain qualities that make you uncomfortable or that you're not proud of. It's important to approach these with the same level of acceptance and understanding as the rest. Treat yourself with kindness and compassion, just as you would a best friend.
- Consistency is key in journaling exercises. Regular practice will make the process of self-acceptance become second nature and the more frequently you do it the more you'll benefit.
- Take some time to reflect after each session. Try to understand

what each trait means to you and how it affects your life and relationships. This understanding can offer valuable insights into your personal growth journey.

- This journey towards self-acceptance and unconditional self-love is not a sprint; it's a marathon. Be patient with yourself and remember that meaningful change takes time.
- Be open to surprises. You may discover qualities about yourself that you didn't know existed. Embrace them, accept them and learn from them.
- At the end of each session express gratitude. Be thankful for your courage to undertake this journey, for your honesty and for the insights gained. Gratitude can powerfully enhance your overall emotional well-being.
- Remember to celebrate your progress, no matter how small. Each step towards self-acceptance is a victory.
- If you feel comfortable, consider sharing your experience with someone you trust. They might provide a new perspective or insights that you may have missed.
- Unconditional self-love is a journey of self-exploration, acceptance and compassion. Treat this exercise as a gift to yourself, a space where you can explore and embrace who you truly are without fear of judgement or criticism.

Ex**ercise 2: Forgiveness Meditation**

This exercise helps you cultivate forgiveness towards yourself for past mistakes or perceived shortcomings. Forgiveness is a crucial element of unconditional self-love, as it enables you to release past guilt and resentment that might be preventing you from fully loving yourself.

Instructions

- Start by finding a quiet and peaceful space where you will be undisturbed. Ensure that you're in a comfortable position, whether sitting or lying down.

- Before you begin the meditation set an intention. It could be something like, 'I am here to forgive myself and let go of past guilt.'
- While this step is optional, a guided forgiveness meditation can be helpful, especially if you're new to meditation. There are many free guided meditations available online and many meditation apps that offer specific forgiveness meditations. Choose one that resonates with you.
- Start your meditation by taking a few deep breaths, in through your nose and out through your mouth. This can help you relax and focus your mind.
- As you meditate, bring to mind past mistakes or instances where you're holding on to guilt or regret. Visualise yourself in that situation. Instead of indulging in negative emotions, offer yourself words of forgiveness and understanding. Remind yourself that everyone makes mistake and it's through these mistakes that we learn and grow.
- See the resentment and guilt leaving you as you exhale. With each breath you're letting go of these negative emotions.
- End your meditation with an affirmation of self-love. It may be something like, 'I forgive myself,' 'I accept myself,' and 'I choose to love myself unconditionally.'
- After the meditation take a moment to note how you feel. Are you lighter, calmer or more at peace? Write your thoughts and feelings in your journal.
- Practice this forgiveness meditation regularly. You might choose to do it daily, weekly or simply whenever you are burdened by guilt or resentment.
- Remember, the goal of this meditation is not to forget past mistakes or dismiss them but to forgive yourself for them. Practicing self-forgiveness is key to emotional healing.

Additional Guidance

- Stay present during your meditation. It's natural for your mind to wander, especially when you're recalling past mistakes. Gently guide your focus back to the practice when this happens.

Mindfulness will help you engage fully with the process of forgiveness.

- As you forgive yourself, remember to show empathy. Consider the circumstances that led to the mistake. Acknowledge that you did the best you could with the knowledge and resources you had.
- Approach your past self with non-judgment. Recognise that everyone makes mistakes and that it's part of being human. Remember that mistakes are opportunities for learning and growth.
- Use visualisation to enhance your meditation experience. Imagine guilt and resentment leaving your body with each exhale and being replaced with forgiveness and love on each inhale.
- Forgiving yourself may not come easy and can take time. Be patient with yourself throughout the process.
- Consistency is key to cultivating forgiveness. Make this meditation a regular part of your routine to reap its full benefits.
- Give yourself time to process your feelings after each session. Write about your experiences in a journal to aid in reflection and understanding.
- Try seeking help from a counsellor if self-forgiveness is difficult. They can provide guidance and techniques to navigate through your feelings.
- Use positive affirmations not only during the meditation but also in your daily life. They can serve as reminders of your commitment to self-love and forgiveness.
- Ensure you rest after the session. Forgiveness can be emotionally draining, and resting allows your body and mind to absorb the positive effects of the meditation.
- Forgiveness is not about erasing or minimizing your past mistakes but recognizing them, learning from them and releasing the negative emotions associated with them. This exercise is a crucial step towards achieving unconditional self-love and emotional healing. Be gentle with yourself as you embark on this journey.

Exercise 3: Reflect on Your Dog's Love

This exercise aims to harness the profound lesson of unconditional love that our dogs offer us. By reflecting on your dog's love you can gain insights into how to apply the same non-judgemental and accepting love towards yourself. You will need a notebook or journal for this exercise.

Instructions

- Start by finding a calm and peaceful location where you won't be disturbed. If possible, have your dog with you during this exercise.
- Spend a few moments quietly observing your dog. Notice their loyalty, their happiness to see you, their trust in you and their unconditional love, regardless of the circumstances.
- Reflect on this display of love. Think about how your dog loves you unconditionally. They don't care about your appearance, job, bank balance or your mistakes. Their love is not diminished if you're having a bad day or if you didn't achieve your goals.
- Now, consider how you can apply this unconditional love to yourself. Think about how it would feel to love yourself in the same way your dog loves you, without conditions, judgement or expectations.
- Write your reflections in your journal. Write about your observations of your dog's love, your feelings about it and how you can implement this kind of unconditional love in your relationship with yourself.
- Create an affirmation that encapsulates this lesson of unconditional self-love. Try something like, 'I deserve to love and be loved unconditionally, just like my dog loves me.'
- After this exercise, take a moment to reflect on how you feel and write your thoughts and feelings in your journal.
- You can practice this reflection as often as you wish. You may find it particularly beneficial during challenging times when self-love may seem difficult.

- This exercise is a reminder that just as dogs don't judge us based on our mistakes or flaws, we, too, deserve that same grace and acceptance of ourselves. After all, to heal we must first learn to love ourselves unconditionally.

Additional Guidance

- Throughout this exercise be fully present with your dog. Notice their behaviours, expressions and the love they radiate. Immerse yourself in the experience of observing and connecting with them.
- Express gratitude for the unconditional love your dog shows you. Reflect on how their love has affected your life, and express appreciation for their presence and companionship.
- Take the time to reflect on the lessons your dog's love teaches you. Consider how you can apply that same non-judgemental and accepting love towards yourself. Explore any self-limiting beliefs or conditions you've placed on self-love and challenge them.
- Close your eyes and visualise yourself loving and accepting yourself unconditionally, just as your dog does. Imagine a warm, nurturing light filling your being as you embrace self-love and acceptance.
- When writing in your journal be authentic and vulnerable. Don't hold back from expressing your true feelings and insights. This exercise is a personal exploration, and your journal is a safe space to be honest with yourself.
- Incorporate this reflection into your routine regularly. Reflecting on your dog's love and applying it to self-love is an ongoing practice. The more you engage with it the more profound and transformative the effects will be.
- As you reflect, practice self-compassion. Be gentle with yourself and embrace any vulnerabilities or insecurities that arise. Treat yourself with the same kindness and understanding that your dog shows you.
- Identify practical steps you can take to practice self-love and acceptance in your daily life. This may well include affirmations,

self-care practices, setting boundaries or seeking support when needed.

- Take the lessons from this exercise to use in your interactions with others. Practice offering non-judgemental and accepting love to those around you, mirroring the unconditional love you receive from your dog.
- Celebrate your progress along the journey of self-love and acceptance. Acknowledge the small victories, moments of growth and acts of self-compassion. Each step you take is significant, and celebration fuels further transformation.
- Remember, this exercise is a gentle reminder that you deserve love and acceptance without conditions, just as your dog loves you. Embrace the lessons they teach you ,and carry the warmth of their unconditional love with you as you cultivate self-love and acceptance.

❋ ❋ ❋

CHAPTER 2: LOYALTY

The loyalty of dogs is undisputed, and Harvey was no exception. I knocked on the door but there was no answer. She had only phoned me half an hour ago asking me to go round to her home. The door was unlocked; maybe she was in the garden. As I walked through the living room I saw her asleep on the sofa. I was relieved, thankful that she was resting. I noticed Harvey, wide awake, with a look of such worry in his eyes, his whole body upright and tense. I immediately knew something was wrong. At that moment the phone rang.

'Hi, it's Alison, sorry Lucy is asleep at the moment. Can I get her to call you back?'

'I need to ask you to wake her up. Now.'

The tone of the community mental health nurse made my heart race with fear. I tried to wake her up. Harvey sensed there was help at hand, and the worry faded from his eyes, yet he did not move from his protective spot next to her side.

'I've called the ambulance. Can you stay with her until it arrives?'

I had been in this position so many times before.

'The only way I can describe it is I need to leave my head somewhere else, but I can't. No matter what I try to do I can't live with the pain.'

My beautiful, sweet, funny and kind friend. The kindest person I know who struggles to get through life. Please, not again, I silently prayed. I hoped that this overdose, one of many, had not done the permanent damage to her body that the doctors warned of.

The ambulance staff were amazing, as always. They had roused her slightly, and Harvey finally settled down in his basket, exhausted but relieved. He knew she was in safe hands now. I looked after Harvey, as I had done before, until she returned home. He was quiet and withdrawn even though we made a fuss of him. A permanent worried frown rested across his forehead, his mind racing with thoughts of Lucy and if she was okay. During the welcome home I laughed at his exorbitant joy. It was like he had not seen her for a month yet it had only been two short days. We both hoped, at least for a while, that she would be safe and would get through the days ahead with Harvey, forever loyal and loving, firmly by her side.

Isn't the loyalty of dogs heartwarming? It's like they've attended a loyalty masterclass and come out top of the class. The ways they show it are endless; the rock-solid commitment, unwavering trust and unfailing faith all paint a picture of loyalty that's rock solid. Do you know what is behind this fascinating trait? Let's travel back in time. Dogs evolved from wolves, and within a wolf pack each member relies on the others for protection, food and company. When dogs became man's best friend they shifted this pack mentality towards us. Suddenly we became their 'pack', their family, and the loyalty they once showed to their fellow wolves they showed us.

This dog human bond is an incredible testament to trust, don't you think? It makes us wonder, *What if we mirrored this beautiful bond in our own relationships? How might our relationships transform if we adopted the same level of loyalty, trust and unwavering faith that dogs show us every day?* Imagine the depth and richness of our relationships if we adopted the dog's pack mentality, looking out for each other, showing up in times of need and displaying our unwavering loyalty, expecting nothing in return. By being there, steadfast and reliable, regardless of the situation. It's a tall order but isn't it one worth striving for? After all, the bond between a dog and its human is one of the purest forms of friendship out there.

Isn't it amazing how in tune dogs are with our feelings? It's as if they're gifted with a sixth sense that allows them to recognise our emotional states, even when we're doing our best to hide them. Have you ever been upset and then found your dog nudging into your side, their eyes filled with concern, as if trying to provide some comfort? Or, on the flip side, have you noticed how they share in our joy when we're on top of the world, their tails wagging so fast they create a breeze? This beautiful connection goes beyond simple response. It's more of an emotional mirroring; they reflect our emotions as if they were their own. It's an unspoken language of empathy and understanding that goes beyond words. When they nuzzle us in times of difficulty or celebrate with us in moments of joy it's as though they're communicating something profound. It's as if they're saying, 'I see you. I understand what you're going through and I'm here for you, no matter what.' Isn't that a beautiful display of loyalty? It's pure, untainted and free from any ulterior motives. It's a loyalty that expects nothing in return except perhaps a cuddle or an extra treat.

With regard to patience, dogs are in a league of their own. Imagine this: You've been out all day, buried in work, the usual daily grind, and who's there when you return home, tail shaking like a drummer's sticks during a solo performance? You guessed it, your dog, faithfully awaiting your return. We're not talking about the patience of a dog with nothing else to do; this is a different patience, a unique brand only dogs seem to possess. It's patience that combines keen anticipation with unabashed joy at the very idea of seeing you again. Their day becomes a countdown to your return, every tick of the clock bringing you a second closer. Your arrival? That's the highlight of their day. It's like their favourite band came on stage, only a thousand times better.

The moment you walk through the door you're met with a level of excitement that makes a rock concert look like a library, their tails wagging with such enthusiasm you'd think they're trying to take flight. What's truly heart-warming about this is that it's not only about the excitement of seeing you again but a testament to their undying loyalty. It's as though with every passing minute their certainty of your return strengthens, fuelling their anticipation and deepening their loyalty. Every time you leave and come back it's like you're reconfirming a promise saying, 'See, I told you I'd come back,' and every time their trust in you grows. So when you see your dog waiting for you, remember, it's more than just patience; it's a silent pledge of loyalty and confirmation of the deep bond between you. It's a sign of their unwavering belief in you, a belief that says, 'No matter how long you're gone I know you'll always return to me.'

It's easy to assume loyalty is all about the good times, the belly rubs and the game of fetch on a sunny afternoon, but life isn't always a walk in the park is it? And that's when the remarkable loyalty of your dog truly shines. Whether you're full of life and laughter or slumped on the couch, their loyalty doesn't falter based on your mood or health. It's like they're living out the classic wedding vow, in sickness and in health, only they don't need a ring or a ceremony to commit their silent support. That unwavering loyalty stands as a heart-warming testament to the depth of their devotion to you. Harvey showed this loyalty and commitment to Lucy's well-being time and time again.

Think back to the last time you were under the weather. Remember how your dog seemed instinctively to understand? How they somehow knew it wasn't the time for their usual playful antics but a moment for quiet support? There's something incredibly comforting about having your dog by your side when you're unwell. It's like they transform into this tender-hearted nurse and they stick around, offering their silent support. Not making a fuss, not seeking attention, but just being there. A warm, comforting presence at your side. An occasional nudge of their head into your hand, a soft whimper as if they're saying, 'I'm here for you.' Their whole demeanour seems to change, doesn't it? It's like they've tuned into your emotions, sensing your need for comfort and company. They don't pester you for walks or get restless because playtime has been skipped. They don't back away or hide until you're back on your feet again. No, they stick with you quietly staying by your side, a constant reminder that you're not alone. Harvey got Lucy through those difficult times and was there to enjoy the good times when she became well again.

You might be wondering, *This is all well and good but what's it got to do with me? I'm not a dog!* True, you aren't, but here's the thing. Our dogs are doing something right, something we humans could stand to learn a thing or two from. What is that, you ask? Well, it's their way of life, loyalty, the golden thread that stitches together all of their interactions with us. It's not a part-time show for them; it's ingrained in their everyday actions, in every wag of their tail and every adoring look they give their humans.

What if we were to take a page out of a dog's book? What would it look like to be the human version of a dog's unwavering loyalty? How would our lives be if we were to weave that same golden thread of loyalty into our own relationships? Imagine the bonds we would foster, the friendships we may strengthen and the love we could deepen. Bonds that would weather life's ups and downs and come out stronger on the other side. This is where dogs' demonstrations of loyalty comes in as a powerful lesson. They show us how the bond between a dog and a human can be a masterclass in trust, a beautiful example of how to cultivate and nurture our own relationships.

Trustworthiness is the cornerstone of any strong, lasting relationship, but it's more than just a one-time thing. It's not about making a promise today and forgetting about it tomorrow. Trustworthiness is about being consistent, about proving repeatedly that our actions align with our words. Picture this, you've got a friend, someone you like spending time with. They're always up for a good time, but what about those not-so-good times, the ones where you're fighting an uphill battle? Can you count on that same friend to be there for you? If they prove they're as dependable during the tough times as they are in the good times wouldn't you trust them a lot more?

That's what trustworthiness is all about. It's about demonstrating, time and again, that you're the sort of person who sticks to their word, no matter what. That you're not only there for the laughs and good times but also for the tears and challenges and once people see that, once they realise that they can depend on you in sunshine and the rain, that's when you've built a rock-solid foundation of trust. It makes people feel safe and secure around you, knowing they can rely on you. They see you as someone who's got their back, someone who'll stand by them through thick and thin and that trust, that reliability, becomes the bedrock of a strong, enduring relationship.

This is not only about physical safety, although dogs are great at that too. This is about emotional safety, about giving you a space where you can be your authentic self, with no fear of judgement or rejection. This is about providing a sanctuary where you can express your thoughts and feelings freely. It's about ensuring you are seen, heard and accepted for who you are. When you're around someone who's genuinely loyal, someone who's there for you no matter what, there is a sense of relief. It's like you can finally let your guard down and be yourself. That's because loyalty creates a sense of emotional security. It helps us build trust, fosters open communication and deepens our connections.

What if we borrowed this gentle, attentive, comforting behaviour and offered it to the people in our lives? Imagine the depth of connection we would create. We could become the person people open up to, to share their thoughts, dreams, worries and their fears. This goes beyond just being a shoulder to cry on. It's about validating their feelings, acknowledging their experiences and letting them know that what they feel is important. Like a loyal dog is a constant in its human's life, we can be a constant in the lives of those around us. We can be the one who listens, understands and validates. We can be the one who makes sure others are heard, seen and cherished. In doing so, we can nurture a sense of unity, of togetherness, which is invaluable in our often divided world.

Loyalty does double duty, as it's also a powerful launchpad for personal growth. Think about it this way. When you're lounging on your sofa, sharing your day with your dog, they're not just there mindlessly wagging their tail but helping to create your safe space, a source of comfort, where you can spill your thoughts and feelings without a worry in the world. But how does that tie in with personal growth you ask? Well, consider this. What if your relationships, built on the same loyalty that your dog shows you, become your personal mirrors? These relationships can help us see ourselves as we truly are, warts and all. Share your fears, dreams, failures and triumphs with someone who's loyal to you. Picture them genuinely listening to you, truly understanding your experiences, deeply caring about your feelings. They listen, understand, care and reflect back at you. They're not afraid to hold up that mirror and show you what you might not see. They highlight your strengths, draw attention to your weaknesses and, above all, encourage you to be the best version of yourself.

In this kind of trust-filled, open and honest space you're free to be your authentic self. You can acknowledge your victories, no matter how small, and truly celebrate them. At the same time you can face your weaknesses, not with judgement but with acceptance. The understanding that we're all works in progress is liberating. It also motivates us to strive for improvement. We become eager to grow, develop, learn from our mistakes and to be better than we were yesterday. So, let's make the most of these loyal relationships and use them as our mirrors to self-awareness, catalysts for change and stepping-stones to becoming the best versions of ourselves. Let’s see ourselves as dogs see us: worthy, lovable and capable of growth.

To value the loyalty masterclass we receive from dogs I encourage you to embrace the exercises and reflections to cultivate loyalty in your relationships. The loyalty that dogs exemplify is not only a characteristic unique to them but also a lesson they're teaching us. Take a moment to reflect on how dogs show their loyalty to us, from their unwavering presence during both the highs and lows of our lives to their ability to create an emotional safety net. They teach us the power of trust, empathy and being a constant source of support for those we care about. When you cultivate loyal relationships they become mirrors that reflect your true self and offer opportunities for self-awareness and improvement. Allow these relationships to motivate you to become the best version of yourself, continually learning and growing. Let loyalty become a guiding principle, a foundation for trust, unity and personal growth. By doing the exercises laid out in this chapter, you will not only deepen your understanding of loyalty but also infuse its essence into your own life. Here's to living with a little more 'dog' in us and a lot more loyalty.

* * *

Exercise 1: Building Trust Through Reliability

The goal of this exercise is to build trust, a key ingredient of loyalty, by improving your reliability.

Instructions

- Start by identifying the commitments you make in your daily life. These may be anything from work deadlines, meeting friends, completing household chores or self-care routines. Record these commitments and keep them in a place where you can see them regularly.
- Not all commitments carry the same weight. Identify which commitments are the most important to you, and to those who are relying on you, and rank them in order of their importance.
- One of the main reasons we break our promises is because we often overestimate what we can realistically achieve. Make sure the promises you make align with your abilities and time. When in doubt it's better to under-promise and over-deliver.
- For each commitment make a plan that includes when and how you will fulfil it. Include contingencies for potential obstacles you might face.
- The most crucial step is to follow through with your plans. If you cannot, for any reason, let the other person know as soon as possible and renegotiate your commitment.
- At the end of each week review your commitments and your success in meeting them. Celebrate your successes and identify areas where you fell short. Reflect on what went wrong and how you can improve.

Additional Guidance

- Remember, the goal is not to be perfect but to improve. Everyone slips up sometimes, but the key is to keep striving to be more reliable.
- Be patient with yourself. Building trust takes time and consistent effort.
- It's equally important to communicate openly with those you're making commitments to. If you realise you can't fulfil a commitment let them know, giving them as much notice as possible.

- As you become more reliable, you'll notice that people's trust in you will grow, reinforcing your relationships with a strengthened sense of loyalty.

Exercise 2: Fostering Loyalty Through Open Communication

The aim of this exercise is to develop loyalty by adopting open and honest communication in your relationships. This exercise, when done regularly and mindfully, can foster a deeper level of understanding and trust in your relationships, leading to stronger bonds of loyalty.

Instructions

- Decide on a specific time each week to have open conversations with the people in your life. It could be a casual chat over dinner, a scheduled phone call or a dedicated meeting. The aim is to create a safe space where you can both express yourselves freely.
- Before your conversation, take some time to reflect on what you want to discuss. Consider your feelings, thoughts, aspirations and concerns. Being clear about what you want to express will make the conversation more productive.
- During your conversations make sure you practice active listening. This means fully focusing on the speaker, avoiding interruptions and providing thoughtful responses. This not only shows respect but also encourages the other person to share more openly.
- While it's important to be respectful and considerate, try to express your thoughts and feelings honestly. It's okay to show vulnerability. Authenticity often invites authenticity in response, which can strengthen the bond of loyalty.
- If there are issues that need to be addressed provide feedback in a constructive manner. Use 'I' statements to express your feelings, such as 'I feel upset when...' rather than 'you always...' This approach makes the conversation less accusatory and more open to resolution.

- After each conversation reflect on what was said, how it was said and how it made you feel. Consider what went well and any improvements for next time.

Additional Guidance

- Remember that open communication isn't just about speaking; it's equally about listening and understanding.
- Keep in mind that everyone has their own communication style. Be patient and flexible in your approach.
- Honesty should never be an excuse for unkindness. Be honest but also considerate of the other person's feelings.
- Consistency is key. Open communication needs to be a regular practice to have a meaningful impact on your relationships.

Exercise 3: Building Loyalty Through Respecting Boundaries

The goal of this exercise is to enhance loyalty by understanding and respecting each other's boundaries. Respecting boundaries can significantly improve your relationships, leading to a deeper sense of loyalty and mutual respect.

Instructions

- The first step is to understand your own boundaries. These can be physical, emotional or even time boundaries. Reflect on what makes you uncomfortable, what you need for your well-being and where you draw the line.
- Once you clearly understand your boundaries, communicate them to the people in your life. Be clear, direct and assertive. Remember, it's okay to say no when a boundary is being crossed.
- Ask others to express their boundaries as well. Make it a safe and open conversation where they can comfortably state their comfort zones, personal space and needs.
- Actively respect these boundaries. This means refraining from behaviours that cross these lines and addressing your actions if

you inadvertently cross a boundary.

- Boundaries are not always static and can change based on experiences and circumstances. Regularly check in with the people in your life to ensure the boundaries set are still relevant and respected.

Additional Guidance

- The key to this exercise is open communication and mutual respect. In addition to setting boundaries it's also about ensuring they are respected consistently.
- It's important to be patient with yourself and others during this process. Understanding and respecting boundaries can take time and practice.
- Ensure you approach these conversations with empathy and understanding. Everyone has different needs and comfort levels, and these should be respected.
- If a boundary is crossed, address it immediately and openly. This helps prevent resentment from building up and strengthens the relationship by enhancing trust.
- Remember, boundaries are not restrictions but guidelines that ensure everyone involved in a relationship is valued and comfortable.

* * *

CHAPTER 3: FORGIVENESS

Harvey, Tiny and Toby, the dogs that treasure us as much as we do them. They make a house a home. They love and heal us, make us laugh and make us cry. They experience fear and they hurt as we do. Harsh words, raised fists and kicks. Often they choose to stand in harm's way, ready to protect at all costs. I read out the risk assessment form, pausing briefly before asking, 'Is he cruel to animals?' 'Yes, he kicks the dog, he burnt our rabbit, he drove off with the cat and dumped her miles away.' I never became immune to the stories I heard while working for a domestic abuse charity on their helpline. I believed passionately in what I did to empower woman to believe in themselves and offered practical support to help them break free from abusive relationships, but pet foster placements were scarce, and pets continued to be a barrier to people finding safety.

'But I have two dogs, can they come with me to refuge?'

'I can't leave them with family or friends; he knows where they live and will cause problems.'

'The cat will not be safe if I leave. He will not feed it.'

'He will be so angry if I leave; he will threaten to hurt my dog if I do not return.'

'The children will be heartbroken if our temporary accommodation does not allow animals. They have lost so much already.'

'She is all I have, we have been through so much together, I can't lose her.'

I had been in the job for nearly two years and had heard enough to know that I needed to act. It led to the creation of a volunteer group who offer a safe refuge for pets in my area.

It was not only because she was our first foster dog, but there was just something about her that made her special. Our policy is to assess a dog for any issues that may be present because of the abusive environment they had come from before we hand them over to foster parents. She was only seven months old and had already experienced a traumatic life at the hands of her owner's partner. I was expecting a small dog, but she was the biggest puppy I had ever seen. She sat in our living room, back turned to us, pushed as hard up to the door as possible, face down in the corner thinking, *If I can't see them then, hopefully, they can't see me.* We carried on quietly chatting on the sofa, not paying her any attention, with a bowl of food and some water left on the floor close to her and far enough away from us.

Tentatively she risked a look over her shoulder and eventually turned to face us. We carried on and did not make a fuss. The tempting aroma of food encouraged her to move away from the door. As she ate, eyes always raised towards us, just in case, her tension eased. Still not sure, with some small growls made under her breath, she cleaned the dish of food. She gazed at me with the softest hazel eyes, the look of longing to love and trust us in total contrast to the warning growl. Before we went to bed we settled her in her basket, filled full of hand crocheted blankets made by one of our lovely volunteers and wondered what the next morning would bring. The next morning I tentatively opened the door. Not a puddle to be seen.

'Good girl, aren't you clever!'

I held a treat in my hand and carefully stretched it out towards her. She delicately accepted the peace offering and I saw that spark of trust in her eyes grow and a slight wag of the tail as if to say, *I think you are going to be okay*. The difference twenty-four hours can make is remarkable. That first night there was no sign of the playful puppy, but now she was back with a vengeance. Nothing was safe. Everything was to be tasted, chewed, hidden, stolen and played with. My first slobber kiss was gorgeous and it turned out this was her favourite way of letting you know she was happy, which was 99.9 percent of the time. That is the beauty of dogs. No matter what they have been through their ability to forgive, let go of the past and live each day filled with joy is wonderful and a lesson to us all in the art of forgiveness and gratitude. I was discussing with my colleague her funny ways, all the cute things she did and her endless capacity for fun, play and trust.

'Just be careful you don't fall in love with her.'

'It's a bit too late for that I'm afraid.'

The next day we took her to her foster home. I phoned the foster carers before we set off to make sure they were still onboard. They had been slightly hesitant during the first telephone call the previous day when I explained she was a puppy and a big one at that.

'We've been to the shop and got her a bone. We wanted her to have one as soon as she walked in to associate us with food. Oh, and we bought her some toys although not too many yet as we aren't sure how big she is or how sturdy the toys need to be. We've cleared our diaries for the next week, taken down the Christmas tree so it doesn't scare her and made room in our bedroom for the basket. You are still coming today aren't you, we are so excited!'

I laughed, no need to worry about them having second thoughts at all. She had been moved to different homes too many times in her short life, and it was yet another time when she would have to trust more new people. As we loaded her into the crate in the car, my heart sank as I saw her tremble.

'It's going to be okay little one. You are going to spend the next few months with some wonderfully kind people, just you wait and see.'

I reassured her, as we all sat in the living room at the foster house, that these were good people. She kept looking up at me and I nodded over at her new mum and dad and smiled. She quickly devoured the bone they had bought. *Mmm, maybe this place is not too bad.*

'I have to be honest and tell you the good and not so good. She is lovely, gorgeous, house-trained, endless fun and such a joy to be with. She will make you laugh all day. She is also very smelly, breaks wind endlessly when she is excited which is all the time, steals anything she can get her paws on and gives very slobbery kisses. Oh yes, and when she sees a bird she wants to eat them immediately.'

They had put a new dog mat in their living room next to the sofa for her to settle on and explained their policy of not having her on the sofa. They said they would put her basket up in the bedroom for the first night. She was comfortable enough to play with the tennis ball they had bought her before I left. I was already missing her but knew she would be safe in her lovely new home.
I phoned up the following morning with my fingers crossed. I really wanted this placement to be okay, not sure she could cope with another move.

'So, how did the first night go?'

'She did not want to settle in her basket and jumped on the bed. We said no and put her back down, but she just jumped up again. We were both tired so decided that it was fine for her to sleep on the bed, just not under the covers. I got up to use the toilet at 5.00 am and she did not move. I knew she was still asleep as she was snoring, which she did all night. The alarm was set for 8.00 am and I had to wake her up to go out for a wee. I think she was tired from the two long walks we took her on yesterday, and I think the fridge game wore her out. She loves rolling the tennis ball under the fridge and cooker and then watches my husband get on his hands and knees to get it out again for her. By the way, can you hear her now? She is on her back with all her legs in the air having a good back rub on the carpet. You were spot on about the slobbering kisses. I got covered in them this morning in bed.'

Perfect.

A dog's ability to forgive is nothing short of extraordinary. They have this incredible ability to let go of past hurts and move forward, not weighed down by grudges or resentment. Consider a dog that's been rescued from a tough situation, whether it's neglect or abandonment. It's heart-breaking right? And yet, after some time in a loving, safe environment they show signs of trust again. It's as if they've hit the reset button and decide to give humans another chance. They forgive, not just once, but again and again, displaying an astounding capacity for love and trust. How many of us can say we would do the same if we were in their position?

This ability of theirs is like a masterclass in forgiveness. It teaches us that holding onto grudges or resentment doesn't do us any good. In fact, it just keeps us trapped in a cycle of negativity, unable to move forward. But forgiveness, now that's the key to freedom. It's the act of consciously letting go of past hurts and choosing to focus on the here and now. Dogs live entirely in the present. They don't hold on to past hurts or worries about the future. They forgive, forget and move on, living each day as a brand-new adventure. By doing so, they invite more joy and fulfilment into their lives. It's as if they're saying, 'Why waste time holding grudges when there's so much life to live and love to give?' Imagine if we could take a leaf out of their book and approach life with the same spirit of forgiveness.

The way dogs forgive is nothing short of inspirational. They don't keep a mental list of every mistake and don't hold it against you if you step on their tail by accident. Dogs don't bear grudges and don't hold on to the past. They're a lot more focused on the present moment, on the here and now. Picture this: You accidentally step on your dog's tail and they yelp out in surprise and pain. What happens next? Do they growl at you, hold it against you? No, more often than not they're back at your side in no time, wagging their tail, looking at you with those loving eyes, ready to forgive and forget.

Imagine if we could develop that same ability to forgive so quickly and wholeheartedly. If we could let go of the past, stop reflecting on our mistakes and instead focus on the present. What a difference it would make. We'd be freed from grudges, guilt, and ready to fully embrace the present moment. Adopting a dog-like approach to forgiveness could lead to a life that's so much lighter and more fulfilling. So, the next time you see your dog wagging its tail happily, even after you've scolded them or stepped on their tail, remember the lesson they're teaching you. Live in the now, forgive quickly and love unconditionally.

The whole process of forgiveness is like embarking on a transformative journey, one that has the potential to change not just our outlook but our entire life for the better. When we hold on to resentment it's like carrying a heavy backpack filled with bricks. And what does that do? It weighs us down, literally and metaphorically. It's as if we're hiking up Mount Everest and with every step that backpack of bitterness becomes a little heavier, making the climb that much harder. But dogs have this whole forgiveness thing worked out. They know how to drop the bag, shake off the negativity and just enjoy the journey.

Let's say we want to follow their lead, ditch the baggage and embrace the present. What does that look like? Well, first it's important to realise that letting go doesn't mean ignoring what happened or diminishing the hurt. It's not about giving a free pass to those who have wronged us. It's about acknowledging what happened, understanding how it affected us and then making a conscious decision to let go of the bitterness, resentment and anger.

Picture yourself standing at the edge of a clear still lake, the surface as smooth as glass. You're holding a small stone which symbolises a negative emotion you've been carrying around. Now take a deep breath, imagine the stone in your hand, then you let it go by skimming it across the lake. Watch as it breaks the surface of the water, creating ripples and then sinks. It's out of your hands now, no longer your burden to carry. You've acknowledged it, you've let it go and now you're free to enjoy the serene beauty of the lake. Or imagine standing in a beautiful meadow or on a golden beach holding a balloon. As you breathe, out picture all your negative emotions flowing out of you and into the balloon. Let go of the balloon and watch as it floats away into the sky, taking your burdens with it, leaving you light and free. You've not only acknowledged your feelings but you've also let them go.

To truly forgive, we need to do what dogs do. We need to acknowledge our feelings, understand them and then decide to let go. It's about setting ourselves free and living in the present instead of being chained to the past. When we can do this we not only relieve ourselves of an immense burden but we also open ourselves up to the potential for greater happiness and peace. It's a transformative journey, a deeply personal one, but one that promises a brighter, lighter future.

Dogs love us with a heart that is wide open, even with our imperfections and all our mistakes. They don't hold our past mistakes over our heads or expect us to be perfect. In their eyes we are always enough. Can we learn to extend the same kindness and acceptance to ourselves? Just imagine your dog, wagging its tail joyfully, as you walk through the door, delighted to see you, irrespective of any mistakes you may have made that day. Can't we all learn to apply that same unconditional love and acceptance to ourselves? By doing so, we allow ourselves space for growth and leave behind the heavy weight of self-blame, adopting instead a mindset of self-compassion.

Forgiveness and empathy go hand in hand. Dogs, being the masters of empathy, are constantly showing how understanding someone else's perspective, feelings and experiences help foster forgiveness and connection. They don't get bogged down in the 'right and wrong' of a situation; they simply accept and respond with love. Imagine if we could apply that kind of thinking to our human relationships. When we get caught up in disagreements or conflicts what if, instead of digging our heels in and insisting we're right, we paused, took a step back and tried to understand the other person's point of view? By doing this, we give empathy a chance to bridge the gap and diffuse the tension. It's like stepping into their shoes and seeing the world from their perspective. It doesn't mean we have to agree with them, but understanding their feelings and experiences can soften our stance, making it easier to forgive and connect.

Choosing to build bridges instead of walls is more than just a harmonious way to live; it's a path towards deeper, more meaningful relationships. When we build walls we're isolating ourselves and shutting others out, but when we build bridges we're creating pathways for connection, understanding and love. We're saying, 'Hey, I see you, I hear you and I value our relationship more than being right.' That's a powerful message to send, don't you think?

We can be inspired by dogs to unlock the incredible power of forgiveness and let go of past perceived wrongs, creating a more fulfilling present. Their unconditional love and acceptance can inspire us to offer the same kindness to ourselves and others, cultivating a more compassionate world. After all, forgiveness is not just a noble act but also a crucial step in our healing journey, freeing us from the shackles of resentment and allowing us to experience life's beauty more fully. It's time for you to take up this transformative journey of forgiveness. I encourage you to carry out the following exercises so you can reflect upon your feelings, acknowledge the burden of past hurts and let them go. Remember, forgiveness is not a destination but a journey, so take your time and be patient with yourself.

* * *

Exercise 1: Forgiveness Box

The forgiveness box is a symbolic exercise designed to help you let go of resentment and anger. This physical act can often make it easier to mentally and emotionally release past hurts. For this exercise you will need a small box, a piece of paper and a pen. Any type of box will do. Decorate it in a way that resonates with the theme of forgiveness for you.

Instructions

- Before starting the exercise, take a moment to prepare yourself and set your intention. Remember, the act of forgiveness is for your own peace and healing, not for the person who hurt you.
- Choose a quiet comfortable space where you can sit down with your box, paper and pen. You may wish to make this space special or calming, maybe light a candle or play some soft music.
- Think about the people, incidents or even of yourself where you feel resentful or angry. This might be a recent situation or something that happened years ago. Allow whatever comes up to surface without judgement.

- Take the piece of paper and write down what you want to forgive. You can write a name, a situation or emotion, whatever symbolises what you want to let go. This is for your eyes only so be as honest as you need to be.
- Fold the piece of paper and place it in the box. As you do this, visualise yourself letting go of the resentment or anger associated with what you've written. This act symbolises your intention to forgive and to release the emotional burden.
- You can repeat this process for different people or situations or even the same one if the resentment is still strong. Each piece of paper represents your intent to forgive and each time you place it in the box you are consciously choosing to let go of the negative feelings.
- Regularly return to your forgiveness box. You might wish to add more papers or to take some out and burn or recycle them as a symbol of having fully forgiven and released a past hurt.

Additional Guidance

- There's no need to rush the process. If you're dealing with deeply ingrained resentment or hurt, it may take several attempts before you experience a sense of release. That's okay. Forgiveness is a journey, not a destination.
- While writing your resentments, try to stay present and mindful. It might be painful to revisit these experiences, but the goal is to recognise and confront your feelings in order to let them go.
- Don't forget to extend this act of forgiveness to yourself too. We all make mistakes, and it's important to forgive ourselves for our own shortcomings. Write things you wish to forgive about yourself and place them in the box.
- As you place each piece of paper in the box, try to visualise the resentment or anger dissipating. This could be as a colour, symbol or any visualisation that works for you. This can reinforce the act of releasing the negative emotion.
- Keep the box in a safe but accessible place. Forgiveness is a

process that unfolds over time. As you encounter new challenges or find old hurts resurfacing you can return to your forgiveness box. This isn't a sign of failure but a part of the ongoing journey towards emotional health and well-being.

- Remember, the forgiveness box is a tool to aid your journey, not a magic solution. It may not work for everyone and that's okay. If you find this exercise is not helpful, or if it brings up strong negative emotions, consider seeking professional guidance such as a counsellor or psychologist. They can provide support and alternative strategies for working through resentment and pain.

Exercise 2: Daily Affirmation of Forgiveness

- Affirmations are powerful tools that can help change our thought patterns and attitudes. They are positive statements that, when repeated regularly, can help us create a more positive mindset.

Instructions

- Start by creating a personal forgiveness mantra or affirmation. This should be a positive statement that represents your intent to forgive and let go of resentment. Some examples are: 'I choose forgiveness and release resentment,' 'I can give and receive forgiveness,' 'I let go of past hurts and welcome peace and forgiveness into my heart' or 'Every day I grow in my ability to forgive and let go.' Your affirmation should be in the present tense and speak directly to your heart. It's important that it is true and possible for you.
- Choose a time and place to repeat your affirmation daily. This could be when you wake up in the morning, before going to bed at night or any time that suits you. You may wish to incorporate it into an existing routine, such as while brushing your teeth, during meditation or while taking a walk.
- Repeat your affirmation aloud or silently to yourself. Try to

focus on the words and their meaning. Visualise yourself embodying the forgiveness your affirmation speaks of. You may also find it helpful to place a hand on your heart as you do this to increase the connection to the affirmation.

- Consistency is essential when working with affirmations. Make it a part of your daily routine. Over time, the affirmation will shift your mindset and emotional state towards forgiveness.
- Be patient with yourself. Changing thought patterns takes time. Even if you don't believe or feel the affirmation immediately, continue with the practice. With time you'll notice a shift in your thoughts, feelings and actions towards forgiveness.
- Remember, this exercise is not about forcing forgiveness but about nurturing a mindset that makes forgiveness more accessible. It's a gentle daily nudge towards forgiveness, peace and emotional freedom.

Additional Guidance

- It's important that your affirmation resonates with you personally. Craft your own forgiveness mantra using language and sentiments that are natural and inspiring to you. Remember, it's not just about the words but the emotion and intention behind them.
- You might find it helpful to write down your affirmation and place it where you'll see it frequently, such as on your mirror, refrigerator or computer. Visual cues can serve as reminders to pause and engage with your affirmation throughout the day.
- Whether you're repeating the affirmation silently or aloud try to really mean what you're saying. Emphasise each word, filling them with intention and belief. Over time, this act of conviction can help reinforce your path towards forgiveness.
- Incorporating your forgiveness affirmation into moments of quiet reflection or meditation can deepen its impact. Try repeating your affirmation during these peaceful moments, allowing yourself to fully engage with its meaning and intent.
- Change takes time. Don't be disheartened if you don't

experience an immediate shift in your emotions or mindset. Stick with it and remember that progress may be slow but every step forward is valuable.

- Affirmations are not set in stone. If you sense that an affirmation no longer resonates with you, or isn't helping you progress towards forgiveness, create a new one.
- The goal of affirmations is not to ignore or suppress the past but to help us navigate towards a future with less resentment and more forgiveness. It's a gentle gradual process. As you walk along this path be kind to yourself, recognising that forgiveness is a journey with its own highs and lows. Be patient, stay consistent and believe in your capacity to heal and grow.

Exercise 3: Empathy Building

The aim of this exercise is to foster empathy by stepping into the shoes of the person you feel resentment or anger towards. This helps broaden your perspective and can lead to greater understanding and, ultimately, forgiveness.

Instructions

- Reflect on the situation that caused the negative feelings. Replay the events in your mind, trying to recall as many details as possible. It's important to approach this step with a desire to understand rather than judge or blame.
- Identify your feelings relating to this situation. Are you hurt, betrayed, angry or disappointed? Acknowledge these emotions. Recognise that they are valid and it's okay to feel this way.
- Now, try to step into the other person's shoes. Consider their circumstances and motivations. What might have led them to act the way they did? What could they have been going through at that point in their life? Were there any external pressures that could have influenced their actions? This step isn't about making excuses for them but about understanding their perspective.
- If possible and appropriate consider having an open dialogue

with the person. Ask them about their intentions and feelings related to the situation. This can provide additional insight and aid in the process of empathy building. Only carry out this step if it is safe to do so and ask to have a silent, neutral third party present if necessary.

- Reflect again on the situation but this time from the broader perspective you've gained. Has your understanding of the situation changed? Do you see things differently now?
- Acknowledge that, like you, the person in question is human and capable of making mistakes. Try to cultivate feelings of empathy towards them. Remember, empathy doesn't mean you condone their actions; it simply means you understand their human experience.
- Record your feelings and insights from this exercise. How has this exercise changed your perspective? Are you closer to being able to forgive? Writing it down can help you process your thoughts and emotions. It also provides a record that you can return to and reflect upon as you progress on your journey of forgiveness.

Additional Guidance

- While reflecting on the situation try to remain as neutral as possible. This may be challenging, especially when the hurt is still raw, but it's crucial for gaining an objective understanding of the situation.
- Don't suppress your emotions during this exercise. Acknowledge and express them, either by speaking out loud, writing them down or through some other means of expression.
- Empathy is a deeply personal and subjective experience so don't force it. Allow it to arise naturally from your reflections.
- Communication can be a powerful tool for understanding and forgiveness. However, ensure it's done in a safe, respectful manner. If you believe it might lead to more conflict, it's better to abstain.
- Remember, forgiveness does not mean forgetting what

happened or letting the person off the hook. It's about releasing the burden of resentment for your own peace of mind.

- This exercise may stir up strong emotions. Be gentle and compassionate with yourself as you navigate this process. If this process becomes too difficult to handle alone reach out to a trusted friend, family member or professional for support.
- Keep in mind that empathy and forgiveness are complex processes and it's a journey that takes time. Be patient with yourself and understand that it's okay to go at your own pace. Use this exercise as a tool, but don't forget to look after yourself and seek professional help if needed.

* * *

CHAPTER 4: COMMUNICATION

Madge, my son's grandmother who lived in Yorkshire, did not approve of me. She barely spoke on the phone when calling to speak to Andy, convinced I had deliberately taken her son to live miles away from her, never to be forgiven. She was a strong, no-nonsense Yorkshire woman of few words. She had a whole brood of grandchildren who she adored, and although she didn't see Sam as often as the others, he was, in love if not distance, no further from the others in her heart. He treasures his memories of holidays with her and his granddad, Reg. Cleethorpes and Scarborough, real family holidays. Sam is so lucky to be loved by two sets of amazing grandparents.

By this time, Andy and I had separated and he had moved back up to his roots in Sheffield. I wrote Madge a letter to say thank you for everything she did for Sam and the way she included him in the extended family, grateful that she always reassured Sam that he was always welcome. I did not receive a reply to the letter, not even a phone call. I assumed she had given it a dismissive glance and binned it as was her attitude to me over the years.

Her death a few years ago hit Sam hard. Reg, her husband, had died six months before, and Madge gave up her own health battle, not wanting to carry on without her beloved husband of more than fifty years. Sam was a pallbearer at her funeral and he struggled to hold his shoulders up, straining to bear the weight of his grief, his eyes not wanting to see ahead to her final resting place. He stayed with his dad for a few days and then returned home carrying a small box into the living room. It was a box of items Madge had put aside for him to keep. Precious photos of them together on holidays and family gatherings, Jasper's dog lead and collar, belonging to the dog that Sam had given her, and other bits and pieces. At the bottom of the box was a letter. He read it and passed it to me:

> *Dear Madge, thank you for everything that you do for Sam, I appreciate it so much...*

She had kept that letter for years, putting it in the box that one day she would pass to Sam, wanting him to know that, maybe, she thought his mum wasn't so bad after all. I am thankful she kept the letter, knowing it came from the heart, and regret thinking she had not read it, that it meant nothing. I wish we had got to know each other properly, had more open and honest communication and shared more times of enjoying being with Sam together.

Imagine if we chose to adopt the straightforward, honest communication that dogs use. They have a pure authenticity when it comes to their emotions don't they? Dogs don't muddle their messages with complications or vagueness. If they're happy, they show it with uncontainable enthusiasm, and if they're sad or afraid they'll seek comfort without the need to put on a brave face or pretend everything's okay when it's not. Us humans, on the other hand, we've become masters at disguising our true feelings.

We've got so many unwritten social norms and etiquettes that sometimes it's like we're walking on eggshells, constantly seeking to fit in, avoid offence or protect ourselves from potential harm, but this kind of guarded communication can create confusion and misunderstandings. It can put a strain on our relationships, leaving us disconnected and isolated. If we expressed our emotions as freely and unambiguously as dogs manage to, don't you think it would make our interactions so much smoother and more genuine? It would be like stripping away the masks we wear and just being our authentic selves. It would mean learning to communicate our feelings with sincerity and honesty, being brave enough to show vulnerability, admit when we're scared or sad and to share our joy without fear of judgement. It's about creating an environment of trust where open communication is encouraged and respected.

Dogs are master communicators. Their range of vocalisation is just one aspect of how they communicate. Their barks can be short and sharp or long and drawn out, each conveying a different message. There's the happy 'welcome home' bark, the alarmed 'intruder alert' bark and then there's the insistent 'play with me' whine. It's as if they've got their own language that they're using to chat with us, to make their feelings and needs known. But it's not just the sounds they make that speaks volumes. Dogs are big on body language. A dog's body language is a vibrant form of communication that uses their whole body, from the tip of their tail to the end of their nose. The wag of a tail can mean joy, a relaxed body can signal contentment and a tucked tail and lowered ears can denote fear or submission. They use their body to paint a picture of their internal emotional landscape, helping us understand their feelings and intentions.

Let's not forget about those expressive eyes. Have you ever had a 'conversation' with a dog just by looking into their eyes? It's like they can share their soul with you isn't it? They can convey a sense of trust and love that is incredibly touching or they can show fear or unease. There's truth in the saying, 'Eyes are the windows to the soul.' This holds especially true for dogs. Just imagine if we were as expressive and honest as dogs in showing our feelings through the use our body language to express our emotions with the same level of detail, if we looked into each other's eyes and shared our souls as openly as they do. It's a powerful lesson in authenticity and emotional honesty, and if we take it to heart, it would transform the way we connect and communicate with each other.

Humans, unlike dogs, often fall into the trap of overcomplicating things. Instead of expressing ourselves openly and honestly we hide behind walls of diplomacy, social norms or fear of being judged, which sometimes leads to our true feelings being buried and misunderstood. Can you imagine what a relief it would be to just let go of that? To let ourselves express our emotions openly, without fear of judgement or rejection? When we talk about communicating openly like dogs it's not about venting our feelings recklessly or without consideration for others. Instead, it's about self-awareness and emotional intelligence. It's about recognising what we're feeling, understanding why and finding the right way to express those feelings.

In a way it's like learning a new language, the language of emotional honesty, and just like learning any new language, it takes practice. It involves training ourselves to be more in tune with our emotions and to express them in a way that's respectful to both ourselves and those around us. This kind of open communication encourages deeper connections, breaks down barriers and promotes mutual understanding. It encourages others to be more open with us in return, and it reduces the risk of misunderstandings and conflicts. Imagine the transformation in our relationships if we embraced this kind of open, honest communication. Friends would be more connected, couples' bonds would strengthen and families might find it easier to navigate through tough times together. It starts with us making the conscious decision to open up, express ourselves more honestly and listen with empathy when others do the same.

Emotional transparency is more than just developing healthier relationships; it's about nurturing a more genuine, happier you. Imagine not having to spend energy on maintaining facades or suppressing your emotions. Living life with emotional transparency is like shedding an unnecessary burden: it's like you're finally breathing freely with no weight bearing down on you. Think about it this way. We all have this emotional energy reservoir, and when we spend that energy on pretending, or hiding our feelings, we're essentially depleting our resources for something that doesn't genuinely serve us. It's like spending money on things we don't need; it's just wasteful. But what if we chose to use that energy more productively? What if, instead of suppressing our feelings, we embraced them, understood them and expressed them in an honest and respectful manner? Just think of the freedom that comes from not having to maintain a facade or hide behind a mask.

This kind of emotional honesty can make us feel exposed and vulnerable. It's like we're a dog, rolling over to expose our belly, our most vulnerable spot, but within this vulnerability lies an incredible strength. By allowing ourselves to be seen, truly seen, in all our emotional complexity, we're developing a deeper connection with ourselves and others. Dogs don't worry about looking silly when they roll over for a belly rub. They're not concerned about how others perceive them but just enjoy being genuinely and wholeheartedly themselves. There's a certain strength, a certain courage in that, isn't there? So, if dogs can do it, why can't we? Why not choose to live a more authentic, emotionally enriching life? Yes, it might be scary at first, but the rewards are definitely worth it. You'll be surprised at the joy and contentment that comes from living life in full emotional colour. After all, being true to ourselves is one of the most liberating things we can do. Are you ready to be more dog-like in your emotional honesty?

Dogs communicate their needs so directly, so unapologetically. If they're hungry they let you know. If they want to play, they bring you their favourite toy. They aren't worried about appearing too needy or demanding; they simply express their needs as they arise. It's so natural and instinctual to them. But for us humans it's a whole different story. We're often so concerned about being perceived as needy or demanding we end up suppressing our needs. We're afraid that asking for what we need might lead to conflict, discomfort or even rejection. So, we do this strange dance of dropping hints, hoping that people can read our minds and interpret our needs. But how effective is this strategy really? More often than not it just leads to frustration, misunderstandings and unfulfilled needs.

We often put others' comfort ahead of our own needs. We would rather stay silent than express what we truly want, but in doing so, we're denying our own worth. We're saying, 'Your comfort is more important than my needs.' But why should that be the case? Are our needs not as important? If dogs can ask for what they want with no guilt or hesitation, why can't we? What if we, too, express our needs clearly and confidently, without fear of judgement or rejection? What if we shake off that fear of being labelled 'needy' or 'demanding' and start prioritising our own needs? Imagine how much simpler, how much more fulfilling, our relationships would be if we communicated our needs as straightforwardly as dogs do. It might be uncomfortable at first, and yes, it might lead to some conflicts, but isn't it better to have those tough conversations than to keep our needs locked away? The next time you need something, be it a favour from a friend or some space for yourself, try expressing it directly, as a dog would. You might be surprised at how liberating it feels and how positively people respond to such clear, honest communication. Remember, asking for what you need isn't being needy, it's being human.

This lesson from dogs is simple yet profound. Embrace emotional honesty, express your needs assertively and recognise the value of non-verbal cues. What if we practiced these lessons in our everyday interactions? Could we, like dogs, lead happier more fulfilling lives? Remember, it's not selfish to state your needs; it's essential for your well-being. If you are ready to take a leaf out of your dog's book and embark on a journey towards improved emotional communication and authenticity, I would encourage you to carry out the following exercises.

* * *

Exercise 1: The 'I Feel, I Need' Method

This exercise aims to enhance your ability to express your emotions and needs more effectively and assertively, fostering clear and direct communication in your relationships. You will need a notebook and a pen or any digital device where you can record notes.

Instructions

- Think about a recent situation when you experienced a strong emotion and had an unmet need. What were you feeling? Try to identify the specific emotion. Were you feeling overwhelmed, frustrated, sad or angry? Write this emotion down.
- Next, try to identify what you needed in that situation such as support, understanding, help with a task or simply some time alone. Write this need down.
- Now, construct a sentence using the formula 'I feel ____, I need ____'. Fill in the blanks with the emotion and need you've identified. For example, 'I feel stressed about this project deadline, I need some help to manage my workload.'
- Reflect on the sentence you've written. Does it accurately convey your feelings and needs? Are you comfortable expressing this? If not, think about why that might be and how you can address this.

Additional Guidance

- Try to be as specific as possible, both with your emotion and your need. The clearer you are the easier it will be for the other person to understand and meet your need.
- Keep in mind that the other person also has their own emotions and needs. Be prepared for a conversation and compromise after expressing your needs.
- When expressing your emotion, focus on your feelings rather than blaming the other person. For example, 'I feel ignored when

you use your phone while we're talking' instead of, 'You never listen to me.'

- Practice this exercise regularly. Start with situations where the stakes are low to build up your comfort level. Gradually, move on to more difficult conversations.
- With regular practice the 'I Feel, I Need' exercise can significantly improve your ability to express your emotions and needs effectively, fostering healthier and more satisfying relationships.

Exercise 2: Active Listening Practice

This exercise aims to help you to improve your listening skills and cultivate empathy in your relationships by focusing entirely on the speaker, understanding their perspective and refraining from interruption or unsolicited advice.

Instructions

- Find a partner. This can be a friend, family member or colleague. Explain the exercise to them and make sure they understand and are willing to take part.
- Choose a quiet and comfortable environment for your conversation to minimise distractions. Both of you should be relaxed and open to share.
- Ask your partner to share a story, personal experience or a problem they're facing. They should aim to speak for a few minutes, without interruption. Your task is to listen and only listen. Don't interrupt, don't offer advice and don't start planning your response while they're still talking.
- Pay attention to your partner's body language, facial expressions and tone of voice. These can provide valuable insight into their feelings and emotional state.
- Once your partner has finished speaking, reflect on what you heard in your own words. This may be something like, 'So what I hear you saying is...' or 'It sounds like you're feeling...' Make sure

not to analyse or interpret their words, just reflect them back to show understanding.

- Ask your partner how they felt being listened to in this way. Did they feel understood? What might you improve?

Additional Guidance

- Keep your focus entirely on your partner while they're speaking. If your mind wanders, gently bring it back to the conversation.
- Use non-verbal cues to show you're listening, such as nodding your head, maintaining eye contact or mirroring their expressions.
- Keep an open mind and don't judge the other person's experiences or feelings.
- Allow for pauses and silence. Don't rush to fill the quiet moments. This gives your partner space to gather their thoughts and continue speaking.
- Active listening is a skill that improves with practice. Try to incorporate it into your daily interactions and conversations.
- Active listening is a powerful tool for building deeper connections, fostering understanding, and cultivating empathy. This exercise provides a structured way to practice and refine this skill, enhancing your personal and professional relationships.

Exercise 3: Non-Verbal Communication Awareness

This exercise aims to increase your awareness of non-verbal cues, both from others and yourself, helping you to understand the impact these cues have on your communication and interactions. By observing and adjusting these non-verbal cues, you can foster deeper connections, more empathetic interactions and ultimately more effective and satisfying relationships.

Instructions

- Before you can become aware of non-verbal cues, you need to understand what they are. Non-verbal communication includes body language, posture, gestures, facial expressions, eye contact, physical distance and tone of voice.
- During your daily interactions try to pay extra attention to the non-verbal cues of the people you're communicating with. Are their arms crossed, showing defensiveness? Do they maintain eye contact, showing engagement and interest? What does their tone of voice suggest about their feelings? Make a mental note of these observations.
- Now turn your attention to yourself. How do you stand or sit during a conversation? Are you maintaining eye contact? What tone of voice are you using? Try to become more mindful of your own non-verbal cues and how they might be perceived by others.
- Spend a few minutes reflecting on your observations and write them down. How did the non-verbal cues influence the interaction? What could you do differently to improve your non-verbal communication?

Additional Guidance

- Being fully present and attentive during your interactions will make it easier to pick up on non-verbal cues.
- Non-verbal cues can be subjective and vary between cultures and individuals. Use them as a guide only; don't make assumptions about what the person is feeling based only on their non-verbal cues.
- Like any new skill, the more you practice the more natural it becomes. Try to make this awareness of non-verbal cues a regular part of your interactions.
- Once you become more aware of non-verbal cues you can start using them to improve your communication.

CHAPTER 5: EMPATHY

As I watched the special edition of the Paul O'Grady show, *For the Love of Dogs,* filmed on location in Delhi, I knew that I, too, wanted to go to India to volunteer with a charity dedicated to helping street dogs. His empathy towards animals was huge, and I had similar feelings of compassion, intuitively knowing I needed to do practical things to help ease the desperate situation faced by street dogs. It had been on my bucket list for many years. My partner at the time was not encouraging, not keen to see me fulfil a dream, only choosing to point out the negatives.

'It is not safe for a woman to go to India alone.'

'You will not manage the heat.'

'You're too sensitive and will not cope seeing the level of poverty.'

I did listen but that inner voice, urging me to take this opportunity and follow my dreams, was louder. As I clicked on the confirmation flight details ,I felt nothing but excitement. My mum came to see me off at the airport. As she fussed around, checking I had everything, I gently explained that I was fifty years old and was sure I could manage. I would not change that fussing for the world, full of love and concern, my mum in a nutshell.

I stepped out of the airport in Udaipur, and the heat hit me like a warm blanket. The noise was a heady mix of frantic car horns, people shouting and the frantic bustle of vibrant city life. I hailed a taxi and headed for the hotel. Only a few hundred meters from the airport I saw my first street dog, wandering perilously close to the speeding traffic on the road. My heart rose in my throat, and I sharply caught my breath, adverting my eyes, willingly the dog to move to a safer distance. It appeared the car missed him by inches, but he seemed unperplexed, continuing his search for scraps of food.

Welcome to India, a place like no other. Chaotic dangerous roads, densely populated pavements, the sight of cows wandering freely amongst the pedestrians, the overwhelming stench of rubbish littering the streets and the deafening noise of car horns and shouting. Amongst all this, surviving on their wits, were hundreds of street dogs, searching the rubbish for food, protecting themselves and their puppies from danger, surviving one day at a time. Had I done the right thing coming here? Maybe my doubters were right, that I was just not hardened enough to cope with the sheer numbers of desperately thin and fragile dogs living on the streets. I do not believe that anyone had taken a driving test in Udaipur. Did you need a license to drive a rickshaw?

I had carried out careful research and had decided to volunteer at Animal Aid Unlimited, an animal sanctuary, on the outskirts of Udaipur. It was a short fifteen-minute ride from my hotel, and as most people will probably tell you, your first rickshaw journey is one you will never forget. My head hit the top of the rickshaw as we bumped over the stones on the rough roads outside the city towards the sanctuary. We whizzed by other vehicles with inches to spare, and I was flung from side to side as we sped round corners. I just held on, held my breath and counted down the minutes until we safely arrived.

As I stood outside the sanctuary in the dusty heat, I was filled with so many feelings. Amazement. I had finally made one of my dreams come true. I had to pinch myself, was I actually here? Dread. What sights would I see? Could I cope with the sadness of seeing so many wounded animals? Apprehension. Would the staff think I was useful enough? Would I be able to walk away, fly home at the end of the holiday, knowing my heart may want to stay?

Staff at the sanctuary welcomed me with so much enthusiasm and thanks for my willingness to help that the worry of if I would be of any use vanished immediately. I joined some other travellers who were volunteering that day, and our mutual love for animals ensured we were soon all talking and joking as though we had known each other for ages. Erika, one of the founders of the sanctuary, came to greet us, took us through our induction and allocated us roles.

As I made my way over to the first compound, my eyes rested on a man gently replacing the bandages on a dog's leg. The man was disabled, his legs twisted beneath him, unable to walk. The dog lay patiently before him, sensing he was in safe hands. I could not help but stop and watch as the man's face was filled with something I can only describe as complete fulfilment. It was an act of tenderness so profound that it was humbling to watch. The rawness of emotion this evoked in me was staggering. I had just witnessed an act of pure love delivered with such gentleness. He looked up at me and smiled, and in that moment it was as if the whole universe was smiling. If only because I had witnessed that one moment, my whole trip to India had been justified.

I opened the gate in to the compound and found an old footstool to sit on so that I was only inches from the ground. There were eight dogs in the area, all of them missing a leg, the victims of being hit by vehicles on the chaotic roads where they lived. I opened my arms, rested my elbows on my knees with my hands held wide open and waited. Within minutes, Leoni came to greet me. She was small and sandy in colour. Paralyzed in her back legs she dragged herself along, using her two front legs to move her body. She had the sweetest face, trusting and knowing I was there to help her. She positioned herself under my hands, and I lay them gently on her shoulders. I could feel the warm energy from my hands move through me to her and she gently closed her eyes. I cried. They were not the tears of sadness that I had worried about early that morning but tears of love and gratitude that I could be here, in this amazing place, doing something that I loved. My heart had found a place it could truly call home with people I instantly connected with and understood.

In our modern world where everyone's glued to their devices, chatting through screens and scrolling through social media, it's easy to feel lost, like a tiny boat adrift on a vast digital sea. With all these tools designed to 'connect' us, sometimes, strangely enough, it can feel like we're more isolated than ever. That's why empathy is so important. It allows us to really understand and share the feelings of another, not just on a superficial level but on a much deeper emotional one. It's like we're equipped with these sensors that allow us to tune into other people's emotional frequencies. It's not just about understanding what another person is going through but actually feeling it as if we were in their shoes.

Let's take the example of the Indian rescue centre. Here, volunteers from different backgrounds and different walks of life come together with a shared goal: to provide love, care and a safe space for animals in need. Their shared passion for animals and collective empathy creates an immediate bond between them. It's as if their individual hearts are all playing the same tune of compassion, understanding and unconditional love. It's this empathy, this ability to truly understand and share the feelings of others, that bonds us, forming an invisible web of connection, and it's through these threads of empathy that we weave our relationships, strengthening the social fabric of our communities. Imagine the possibilities if we decided to exercise this superpower more often. How would it change our relationships, our workplaces and our communities? In a world that can often feel so disconnected, empathy can be the bridge that links us together, fostering understanding, acceptance and genuine connection.

Isn't it fascinating how empathy has the potential to transform our interactions, relationships and even our perception of the world? It's like this magical key that unlocks the door to deeper, more meaningful connections. Imagine you're at a crowded party, surrounded by people, but you feel you're on an island, all alone in a sea of laughter and chatter. Sounds familiar, doesn't it? Now, imagine what would happen if you employed empathy. If you took a moment to truly understand the emotions, feelings and experiences of the surrounding people. All of a sudden that sense of isolation melts away. You find common ground, shared experiences and mutual emotions. It's like empathy is this invisible thread that weaves through all of us, connecting us on a profound level. It's not just about understanding other humans, our empathy can extend to animals too. Whether it's the joy you share with your dog when you're out for a run or the heartbreak you feel when you see a homeless dog on the streets, that's empathy in action. By tapping into our empathy we're not just connecting with animals on a basic level, we're also acknowledging their emotions, experiences and their rights to a life free from suffering.

Empathy is a skill, a muscle that we can exercise and strengthen. It's not exclusive to a select few. All of us have the potential to harness this incredible superpower. By making empathy a part of our daily lives, we can build bridges of understanding and compassion in a world that often feels fragmented and disconnected. Whether it's lending a sympathetic ear to a friend or volunteering at an animal shelter, every act of empathy counts. Imagine a world where empathy is the norm rather than the exception, where every interaction is a chance to understand and connect on a deeper level. How much richer and fulfilling would our lives be?

Dogs have this uncanny capacity for tapping into our emotional world. Ever notice how they celebrate when we're exuberant, wagging their tails and hopping about or curl up next to us, mirroring our emotions when we're sad? They seem to almost drink in our emotions don't they? Dogs don't need words to understand us. They're blessed with an emotional radar that's always switched on. It's almost like they're born with the innate ability to empathise. It makes you wonder, couldn't we learn a thing or two from them about empathy?

Dogs naturally show a deep level of empathy. They're not just observers of our emotions but active participants. They share in our joy, sorrow, excitement and our calm. If you're feeling down, they sense it and you might find them nuzzling up to you, providing a comforting presence. If you're excited about something, they'll catch your enthusiasm, leaping around in sheer joy. When a dog is with you, it's completely there with you, in that moment. They're not half-listening while checking their email or scrolling through social media; they're fully present, listening to you with their entire being.

That's the essence of empathy, being fully attentive and emotionally present. When we deeply empathise with the people around us it not only validates their experiences but also strengthens the emotional bond between us. It creates an environment of mutual understanding and respect where love can thrive. In families, empathy could be the missing piece in bridging generational or ideological gaps. It opens up channels of communication, promotes understanding and fosters a sense of togetherness. Each family member becomes more than just a relative; they become a person whose feelings and experiences are understood and valued. Friendships can be elevated to a whole new level and casual acquaintances could turn into meaningful friendships, where each person feels seen, heard and cherished. Empathy is the secret ingredient that turns simple friendships into lifelong bonds, transforming 'me and you' to 'us'. At its core, empathy has a magical element that has the power to transform our relationships, making them more meaningful and fulfilling. Dogs do this instinctively. We can learn from them and cultivate this skill. Imagine how beautiful our lives and relationships would be if we let empathy guide us.

Empathy is not just a personal attribute. Imagine a workplace where every individual truly understands and values the emotions, experiences and perspectives of their colleagues. It's not about just getting the job done but about doing it in a way that respects and considers the feelings and viewpoints of everyone involved. A place where each person feels heard, seen and valued. Empathy in the workplace isn't about indulging every feeling. It's about creating a work environment that promotes open communication, understanding and mutual respect. It's about listening and not just in the traditional sense. With empathy, we don't just hear the words, but we understand the emotions and intentions behind those words. We see the world from our colleagues' perspectives, understanding their aspirations, challenges and concerns. This kind of deeper understanding allows us to respond more effectively, whether it's about making strategic decisions, resolving conflicts or just offering supportive words.

The benefits of empathy in the workplace are far-reaching. A more empathetic work culture boosts morale, fosters teamwork and increases job satisfaction. It makes employees feel valued and respected, which in turn increases productivity and reduces turnover. It's like setting off a positive domino effect where one good thing leads to another. Empathetic leaders inspire trust, loyalty and respect among their team members. They create a sense of belonging and a supportive environment where employees feel comfortable expressing their thoughts and ideas, contributing to the overall growth and success of the organisation. As you can see, empathy is not just a nice-to-have in the workplace; it's a must-have. It's the secret ingredient that transforms an ordinary workspace into an extraordinary one. The kind of place where everyone loves to work and where great ideas thrive.

But what if empathy could not only transform our personal world but also society as a whole? In a world of vast diversity, could empathy help us appreciate the beautiful mixture of our differences? What if, by acknowledging everyone's feelings and experiences as valid, we started seeing the world through their eyes, learning from their narratives? Could this understanding create a more compassionate, inclusive society? Empathy isn't just about understanding others but a key to unlocking ourselves, as empathy extends beyond our interactions with others. It serves as a mirror, reflecting on us, unveiling parts of ourselves we may not have been aware of. As we practice empathy, we explore our own emotional landscape with a newfound understanding as we take an inward journey, a voyage towards self-discovery and personal growth. Through empathy, we not only connect with others on a deeper level, but we also connect with ourselves, becoming more self-aware and emotionally intelligent. Isn't it amazing to think that by understanding others we can also come to better understand ourselves?

Dogs, with their mastered art of empathy, remind us of the power of being fully present, truly listening and sharing joys and sadness. As our teachers they inspire us to infuse empathy into our lives. So how about we take these lessons and apply them to our own lives? I encourage you to carry out the exercises at the end of this chapter. They're designed to strengthen your empathy muscles and truly embed the learning. Step forward, empowered with empathy, knowing that each small step and act of understanding can create ripples of kindness and connection.

* * *

Exercise 1: The 'Why' Game

This exercise fosters empathy by delving deeper into the motivations and circumstances that shape people's actions. To fully benefit from this exercise, you'll need an open and curious mind, willingness to challenge your assumptions and patience to dig deeper beneath the surface.

Instructions

- Begin by recalling a recent incident or behaviour from someone that puzzled or even upset you. Write this incident down, capturing all the details you can remember. It could be anything, a friend cancelling plans at the last minute, a family member's mood swing or a co-worker's unexpectedly harsh feedback.
- Reflect on the incident and ask the first 'why'. For example, 'Why might they have behaved that way?' Write down your initial thoughts or answers. Try to avoid judgement or assumption at this stage.
- Now, dig deeper. Ask 'why' in response to your first answer. If you figured your friend cancelled plans due to work overload your next 'why' could be, 'Why were they overloaded with work?'
- Keep up this process, each time posing 'why' to your preceding answer until you've reached five whys. The idea is to uncover layers of potential motivations or circumstances that you hadn't considered before.
- Look at the chain of whys you've compiled. Does this new perspective help you understand the person's behaviour a bit more? Remember, the aim here isn't to justify or excuse their actions but to foster empathy and understanding.

Additional Guidance

- While playing the 'why' game, make sure you're guided by facts about the person or situation. Avoid unfounded assumptions which may lead you astray.
- If the 'why' trail leads you to a conclusion that make you uncomfortable or challenges your perspective, that's okay. Empathy sometimes involves confronting our biases.
- Remember, this is a process of understanding, not interrogation. Each 'why' should come from a place of wanting to

understand, not assigning blame.

- If the situation allows it, and you feel comfortable, consider having a candid conversation with the person involved. This not only helps you confirm or reject your assumption but also shows your willingness to understand their perspective, an act of empathy in itself.

Exercise 2: Enhancing Empathy Through Non-Verbal Communication

The aim of this exercise is to improve your understanding and interpretation of non-verbal cues. Through observation you will learn to pick up on subtle hints about a person's emotional state. By practicing this exercise regularly, you will hone your observation skills, enhance your understanding of non-verbal communication and strengthen your capacity for empathy. As you become more adept at picking up on non-verbal cues, you'll find that your relationships become deeper and more emotionally attuned.

Instructions

- Pair up with a partner, and choose a quiet location where you won't be disturbed. Sit facing your partner with a comfortable distance between you.
- One person will share a story from their life. This could be about a recent event, a cherished memory or a challenging experience. The other person's role is to listen attentively, focusing on the speaker's non-verbal cues. Pay close attention to the speaker's facial expressions, body language and tone of voice. Remember, the goal isn't to respond to the story but to empathise with the speaker by understanding their emotions.
- After the speaker finishes their story, the listener should reflect on what they observed. What emotions did they perceive from the speaker's non-verbal cues? How did the speaker's body language change as the story progressed? What did their tone of

voice convey about their feelings?

- Now the listener shares their observations with the speaker, providing feedback about what they perceived from the speaker's non-verbal cues. Remember to provide feedback in a respectful and understanding manner.
- After the feedback phase, switch roles and repeat the process. The listener becomes the speaker, sharing a story from their life, while the former speaker turns into the listener, observing non-verbal cues.

Additional Guidance

- Maintain a respectful non-judgemental attitude throughout the exercise. This is a safe space for everyone to share their experiences and emotions.
- As a listener, remember to stay fully present. Avoid the urge to think about your response or get distracted by your thoughts.
- If you're uncertain about an observation, you can ask for clarification. For example, you might say, 'I noticed that your hands were shaking as you shared that part of your story. Could you tell me more about how you were feeling then?'
- As a speaker, try to be as genuine as possible. This exercise isn't about performing or making an impression; it's about practicing empathy and understanding through non-verbal cues.
- Remember that interpretation of non-verbal cues can vary depending on cultural, personal or contextual factors. It's important to maintain an open mind and to respect different perspectives.

Exercise 3: Empathy Bootcamp

This exercise builds and develop your empathy skills. Starting from simpler empathetic responses you will be steadily challenged to empathise in more complex situations.

Instructions

- Week 1 - Self-Empathy. Spend ten to fifteen minutes each day reflecting on your feelings and emotions and record these in your journal. What were the high and low points of your day? How did you react? Were there moments when you could have been more empathetic towards yourself? When you encounter difficult emotions take a moment to acknowledge them. Show yourself compassion and understanding, just as you would do for a friend.
- Week 2 - Empathy in Daily Interactions. Choose one interaction each day where you'll focus on practicing empathy. It could be with a barista, a colleague or a family member. During these interactions, focus on understanding the other person's perspective. Pay attention to their words, tone and body language. After the interaction jot down your observations in your journal.
- Week 3 - Empathy in Challenging Situations. Identify a challenging situation that you're likely to face this week. It might be a difficult conversation, a stressful work meeting or a family disagreement. During these challenging situations, strive to stay aware of your own feelings and those of others. Practice understanding and communicating your understanding. After the event, reflect on your performance in your journal.
- Week 4 - Empathy with Difficult People. Identify a person you find difficult to empathise with. It could be because they have a different point of view, a challenging personality or because of past disagreements. Attempt to understand this person's perspective better. Have a conversation with them, listen to their point of view and show empathy. Afterward, record your experiences in your journal.

Additional Guidance

- Regular reflection on your progress can be extremely beneficial. Take some time each day to write about your experiences and the progress you have made.
- Don't rush the process. Empathy, like any other skill, takes

time to develop. It's okay if you find some stages more difficult than others.

- Remember to maintain a non-judgemental attitude throughout this exercise. This will help create a safe space for empathy to thrive.
- Be patient and kind to yourself. There may be days when practicing empathy feels hard, and that's okay. Keep going and remember that progress is often slow but steady.
- Challenge yourself but also know your limits. It's important to take a step out of your comfort zone, but don't push yourself too hard all at once.
- By steadily practicing empathy, starting from simpler situations and gradually moving to more complex ones, you'll become better at understanding and sharing the feelings of others.

* * *

CHAPTER 6: MINDFULNESS

Do you have a special place that inspires you, where you feel at peace, where you feel connected with something far bigger than yourself? Do you feel peaceful or energised when you visit a favourite city or country? My special place is the sea. It has an ability to resonate at a soul level and soothes me in an instant. It makes me feel thankful for the earth's healing power and for the beauty found in the natural world.

There was nothing particularly remarkable about that day. Nothing to show me that booking the holiday would be the catalyst that would change the whole course of my life. It had all the hallmarks of potentially being a disaster. Two-fifteen-year old lads and me, on holiday in Majorca for a week. I had booked the holiday on impulse, sensing the need to escape to the sun. The relationship I was in at the time was challenging and I needed some time to reflect on my future. The problem was I had little money so it would have to be a last minute, hotel destination unknown, type of holiday. As I clicked the PAY NOW button, I felt excited and nervous. I was taking my son and his friend with me, both fifteen years old and always up to mischief. What could possibility go wrong?

The heat of the sun hit us as soon as we stepped off the plane. The boys slipped on their sunglasses and sped off to find our holiday rep, eager to get to the hotel as soon as possible. Our names were called out on the bus as we approached a large hotel a stone's throw from the sea. I breathed a sigh of relief. The gamble had paid off. The hotel was beautiful and exactly what I would have picked myself. The lads were great, and I realised my initial worries about how they may misbehave had vanished. They were old enough to be trusted to do their own thing within the hotel complex and found plenty to do to keep themselves happy. It's funny how my moody teenager became a kid again as he hurled down the waterside, his beaming smile captured perfectly in a photo I treasure.

The weather was perfect that day. The sky was a stunning shade of blue and the sea was warm, still and inviting, the reflection of the sun causing it to sparkle as though it was filled with thousands of diamonds. The lads had set themselves up on the beach, sun-loungers positioned perfectly to capture the sun's rays, headphones plugged in and a plentiful supply of drinks in the cool bag. They would be happy for at least a few hours. It was a normal busy day at the beach. A blue pontoon was positioned out in the sea, and it was filled with excitable children, laughing and squealing with delight as they played. I waded into the water and realised that I could not find a secluded area as it was too busy. *No worries,* I thought, I was simply grateful to be there.

The warmth of the sea felt like the softest blanket touching my skin, and as I made my way farther out, the sensation engulfed my entire body. Heaven. I was still quite close to the pontoon and smiled as I listened to the sound of the children's uninhibited joy as they played. I lay back and floated in the water. I moved my fingers and toes gently to keep afloat as the sea supported my body. And that's when it happened. I felt the heat of the sun on my face and absorbed its energy. I felt the movement of the waves through my body and the beat of my heart connected with their rhythmic ebbs. I closed my eyes and appreciated the sea, with all its greatness, beauty and strength. It was at that moment that everything I thought I knew to be true changed.

I could no longer hear the children. I could no longer sense my body as separate from the sea. I lost all sense of time and space. I could feel the heat and instinctively knew that my soul was filled with this powerful energy. It was at that moment that I had become one with nature. We are as one. There is no separation. We are not alone. How long did this last? I really do not know. It felt like forever, but it may have only been for a matter of moments. I knew, without hesitation, that we are part of something so beautiful, pure and peaceful. Something far greater and wiser than we will ever realise.

I could suddenly hear the children again and realised I had hardly moved from the spot where I had been floating. The water was not deep, and I waded back to shore, totally mesmerised by what I had experienced. I was filled with an immense sense of joy and gratitude that I had never experienced before. The lads were still resting on the sun loungers, earphones in place. I saw a perfume shop on the main road next to the beach and felt myself drawn to enter. There, on special offer in a huge display, was the perfume, Happy, by Clinique. I laughed. Perfect. I bought the biggest bottle they had and now, when I need to remember that day, I reach for my Happy bottle and know it will all be okay. Whenever I find my faith wavering, and I doubt myself and my abilities, I remember that day, the day when I knew that we are all filled with an abundance of wonder and strength that will always support us. It was a moment of mindfulness and complete presence.

Dogs offer us a masterclass in mindfulness. They live their lives with such unabashed joy and presence, having mastered the art of living fully in the present moment. They have this natural ability to shake off their worries and revel in the joy of now. When they're chasing a ball it's not only about catching the ball. It's about the feel of the wind ruffling their fur, the feeling of the grass beneath their paws, the rush of excitement coursing through their veins. They're not concerned about what happens next. They're not dwelling on a past mishap. They're fully, joyfully, unapologetically present. Imagine if we could immerse ourselves so completely in the moment. If we could let go of our regrets about the past and our anxieties about the future. If only we could be here, now, fully engaged with the world. Picture yourself savouring the subtle flavours of your morning coffee, losing yourself in the sound of your favourite song or simply feeling of a gentle breeze on your skin, without the continual hum of thoughts and worries in the back of your mind.

Mindfulness, the practice of being fully present in the moment, is something we often overlook in our fast-paced lives. But dogs? They get it. They show us that life isn't about fretting over what's past or worrying about what's to come. It's about embracing the now, finding joy in the simple pleasures and truly living each moment to the fullest. So, next time you see a dog chasing a ball with utter abandon take a moment to observe them. Notice how they throw themselves into the chase, how they seem to savour every single moment, and remember, that's not just a dog chasing a ball; it’s a masterclass in mindfulness.

When a dog looks at the world, they truly take it in. When you really take a moment to observe a dog you'll realise it's not merely casually glancing around, but it’s totally absorbing the whole environment. It's as if they're decoding the world, one scent, one sight, one sound at a time. They live their lives in full sensory technicolour, not missing a single detail. Take meal times for example. Have you noticed how they approach their food? There's an element of ritual there that we often overlook. It's not about gulping down the food as fast as possible. There's this appreciation, this savouring of each bite, every crunch echoing delight in their world. It's a pure, undiluted form of pleasure that we humans often miss in our rushed, often mindless eating. What if we could infuse our lives with the sense of presence and enjoyment that our dogs display every day? Imagine what it would be like to feel the grass under our feet, not only as a simple surface, but as a living, breathing part of the earth, teeming with life and energy, or to eat a meal, not only for nourishment but for the sheer joy and pleasure it can provide. Mindfulness is about truly being in the here and now, being fully engaged in the present moment. It's about appreciating the world around us and the simple pleasures that it provides.

Dogs have this incredible capacity to live and let go. If you've ever stepped on a dog's tail, by accident you'd know how quickly they recover. There might be a yelp of surprise or a moment of pain, but that's immediately followed by forgiveness and affection. They don't hold grudges or harbour resentment; they get back to living in the moment as if nothing happened. This is a profound lesson in mindfulness for us humans. Dogs treat each moment as a brand new-start, a fresh slate, free from the weight of past incidents. This is in stark contrast to how many of us allow our past grievances or grudges to cloud our present experiences, preventing us from fully embracing what's happening now.

Now think about the sheer, unadulterated joy a dog derives from the simplest things. You throw a stick, and their day is made! Their happiness isn't dependent on grand gestures, extravagant gifts or material wealth. They find happiness in the ordinary aspects of life, whether it's chasing their own tail, playing with a discarded shoe or enjoying lying in the sun. Dogs don't put conditions on their happiness. They don't wait for grand achievements or perfect conditions to feel joy. They find it in the present moment, in everyday life. We often seek happiness in external accomplishments; a promotion at work, a bigger house, a fancier car, but dogs teach us that happiness isn't something you find somewhere else or in the future. It's something that's accessible to us right here, right now. They remind us that we can cultivate our own joy by appreciating the small, everyday wonders of life by learning to let go.

One of the most powerful lessons that dogs teach us about mindfulness is through their unconditional love. It's like they see through to the heart of who we are, without any preconceived notions, labels or judgements. Whether we've had a good day or a bad one, whether we've triumphed or faltered, their love for us remains constant and unwavering. They don't love us because we're successful, and despite our failures, they simply love us just as we are. Doesn't that strike a chord with you?

As humans, we often tend to be quite harsh on ourselves. We set conditions for self-approval, linking our self-worth to our successes and achievements. When we make mistakes or face failures we're often the first ones to criticise ourselves, forgetting that we're human and that it's okay to not be perfect. But look at dogs. Their love for us doesn't falter when we stumble, nor does it increase when we succeed. It remains steady, teaching us the beauty of unconditional acceptance and self-love. They don't judge us based on what we achieve or how we look or what others think of us. They love us for who we are. This is the core of mindfulness. It's about accepting ourselves as we are in the moment, without judgement or criticism. It's about acknowledging our strengths, weaknesses, successes and failures while still maintaining a sense of self-love and self-respect. Dogs can be great teachers in this regard, constantly reminding us of the power and beauty of unconditional love and acceptance.

Dogs have an amazing ability to stay attuned to their environment. They are masters of observation, alert and responsive to the tiniest shifts in their surroundings. Have you ever wondered how a simple rustle of a leaf or a subtle change in the wind can capture their full attention? Their world is rich with sensory experiences and they miss out on none of it. In contrast, we humans often walk through life in a state of semi-awareness, our minds preoccupied with the past or the future, and as a result, we miss out on the intricate details of the world around us. We overlook the subtle shift in the wind, the rustling leaves, the warmth of the sun on our skin or the simple beauty of a blooming flower. Dogs offer a wonderful lesson here. They encourage us to engage our senses fully, tune in to the present moment and fully immerse ourselves in our surroundings. They remind us to look at the world with wide-eyed wonder, to appreciate the beauty in the mundane and to find joy in the simple act of being alive and present.

Dogs are brave explorers. There's something so inspiring about the way they plunge into new experiences with complete enthusiasm and curiosity. They don't weigh themselves down with worries about what might go wrong, or how things could turn out, but simply embrace the moment as it comes and leap into the unknown. Whether it's a new walk or a squeaky new toy their approach is always the same, excitement and curiosity. There's no room for fear or apprehension, only a sense of anticipation, as they dive headfirst into the experience. Isn't this a beautiful representation of mindfulness at its purest?

Dogs don't just dip their toes in; they dive in the whole way. They teach us to let go of our fears, stop worrying about the 'what ifs' and simply embrace the moment. They show us that it's okay to not know what's around the corner, and it's okay to leap into the unknown with an open heart and mind. That's mindfulness in action, as taught by our dogs. How many times have we, as humans, held ourselves back from truly experiencing life out of fear or apprehension? How often have we let the worry of what might go wrong prevent us from trying something new, or fully immersing ourselves in an experience? Dogs present a different approach to life, one of fearless exploration, being fully in the moment and embracing the unpredictable. They encourage us to approach life with the same enthusiasm, be brave and to dive into the experience.

Reflecting on all these dog traits, it's clear to see that dogs live a life rich in mindfulness. They cherish the present, forgive quickly, find joy in simple pleasures, love unconditionally, remain alert and receptive to their surroundings and embrace new experiences with passion. These are powerful lessons for us, lessons that could transform our lives. What's beautiful is that this wisdom is offered to us every day, in every wag of the tail, every chase after a ball and every contented sigh as they settle down for a nap.

They are living, breathing reminders of the beauty of being fully present.

As we learn from dogs, let's try to cultivate these habits in our lives. Pause and take a moment to relish your meals, truly appreciate the world around you, let go of grudges, find joy in the simplest things, love and accept yourself, stay alert to your surroundings and dare to explore the unknown. With practice, these habits could lead us to a more mindful, fulfilling life. Mindfulness is not a concept we understand purely intellectually. It's a practice, a way of living, which gets better with regular application and conscious effort. Much like how dogs don't merely exist but truly live each moment, it's our turn to take their lessons to heart and put them into practice.

At the end of this chapter is a series of exercises for you to carry out. They are designed to help you integrate the wisdom we've learned from dogs into your daily life. Approach these exercises with the same enthusiasm your dog would approach a new toy or a new walk. Be present, open and patient with yourself. This is not a test but an opportunity to deepen your understanding of mindfulness and enhance your life experience. Some exercises you might find easy while others could be challenging. That's perfectly okay. Remember, mindfulness is a journey not a destination. Don't be disheartened if you struggle initially. Instead, treat each struggle as a dog would, a new experience, a chance to learn and grow. Mindfulness, like any other skill, improves with practice. The more you engage with these exercises, the better you will become at applying these lessons in your daily life. A dog doesn't become an expert at fetching the ball with a single throw, you won't become a master of mindfulness overnight, but with consistent practice, you'll become aware of a gradual shift in your perspectives, reactions and overall well-being.

✻ ✻ ✻

Exercise 1: Mindful Eating

The aim of this exercise is to cultivate mindfulness, enhance our sensory awareness, improve our eating habits and foster a deeper appreciation for our food and the process of eating. It's a simple yet powerful way to turn a daily routine into a practice of presence and gratitude. For this exercise, you will need a small piece of food, such as a piece of fruit, a square of chocolate or a handful of nuts.

Instructions

- Find a quiet place where you won't be disturbed. Sit comfortably and place the food in front of you. Take a moment to breathe deeply, centering yourself in the present.
- Take the piece of food and look at it closely. Become aware of its colour, shape and texture. Are there any spots, ridges or shine on its surface? This isn't about assessing or judging but simply observing.
- Feel the texture of the food with your fingers. Is it smooth, rough, hard or soft? Again, simply note these sensations.
- Bring the food up to your nose and inhale. What does it smell like? Is it sweet, savoury, fruity or something else? Take a moment to appreciate the aroma.
- Take a small bite of the food but don't chew or swallow it yet. Let it sit on your tongue and try to identify the different flavours. Is it sweet, sour, bitter or salty?
- Start chewing slowly, paying attention to the texture changes in your mouth and the different flavours that emerge as you continue chewing. Be aware of how these sensations change with each bite.
- When you're ready swallow the food. Follow the sensation of the food moving down your throat and into your stomach. Sit for a moment and reflect on the experience of eating this piece of food.
- After you've finished, take a moment to appreciate the food you've eaten. How do you feel? Satisfied, content, still hungry?

Additional Guidance

- Try to do this exercise without distractions. Turn off the TV, put away your phone and focus solely on the experience of eating.
- If your mind wanders during the exercise, and it probably will, gently guide it back to the sensation of eating. Remember, this is not a test or a race but a practice.
- Start with a small piece of food, and as you get comfortable with the practice, you can try it with your regular meals.
- Mindful eating is not only about the process of eating but also about the choices you make. Consider where your food comes from, how it was grown or made and the journey it took to get to your plate.
- Remember, the aim is not to judge or critique but simply to observe and experience. This practice is about building a deeper connection with your eating habits and your relationship with food.

Exercise 2: Mindful Walking

This exercise is about promoting presence, increasing sensory and environmental awareness, fostering a mind-body connection and incorporating mindfulness into everyday activities. By consciously engaging with the act of walking you can discover new dimensions of experiences that are often overlooked in our often rushed everyday routines.

Instructions

- Begin by standing still in a relaxed position. Take a few deep breaths and feel the ground beneath your feet. Centre yourself in the present moment.
- Begin walking at a slower pace than usual. This isn't about getting somewhere but rather about experiencing the act of walking itself.
- As you walk, pay attention to the sensation of your feet

touching the ground, the heel-to-toe movement and feel the transfer of weight from one foot to the other.

- Pay attention to your body's movement as you walk. The swing of your arms, the slight rotation of your torso and the balance shift from side to side. Simply be aware of these movements without trying to change them.
- Notice the rhythm of your breath. Is it short and fast or deep and slow? Does it coordinate with your steps? Just observe, don't judge or try to alter your breathing.
- Expand your awareness to include the environment around you. Feel the wind against your skin and hear the birds sing.
- If your mind wanders, which is completely natural, gently guide it back to the sensation of walking and breathing.
- When you're ready to end your mindful walk come to a gentle stop. Stand still for a moment and become aware of the ground beneath your feet and the surrounding environment.

Additional Guidance

- You can perform mindful walking for as short or long a time as you'd like. Even a few minutes can be beneficial.
- Try to embrace a non-judgemental attitude. If your mind wanders or gets distracted, that's completely normal. Gently bring your focus back to the walk.
- This practice is about savouring the experience of walking, not reaching a destination. Don't rush. Allow yourself to move at a slower, more deliberate pace.
- Don't feel limited to only being mindful of the elements listed here. You may also feel the temperature of the air, the scent of the grass or flowers or the colours around you.
- Remember, this is your experience. There's no ‘right’ or ‘wrong’ way to do it. The goal is to be present and aware.

Exercise 3: Five Senses

Often we find our minds are cluttered with thoughts about

the past and worries about the future, making it difficult for us to fully experience the present moment. Dogs don't have these difficulties. They live in the here and now, taking in their environment through their senses, moment by moment. This exercise is designed to help you practice that same degree of sensory awareness. By focusing on each of your five senses, one at a time, you'll learn to tune into your body and environment in a more focused and conscious way. It serves as a tool to help you step out of automatic pilot mode and become an active participant in your sensory experiences.

Instructions

- Find a comfortable position, either sitting or standing. Close your eyes and take a few deep breaths, centering yourself in the present moment.
- Open your eyes and choose one thing in your environment to focus on. Take note of its colours, shape and other visual features. Try not to judge or analyse what you're seeing, simply observe.
- Reach out and touch something within your reach. It could be the fabric of your clothes, surface of a table or the grass beneath your feet. Notice the texture, temperature and other sensations that you feel against your skin.
- Close your eyes again and concentrate on the sounds around you. It could be the hum of an appliance, birds singing outside or the distant noise of traffic. Try not to label or judge the sounds, simply listen.
- Draw your attention to any smells around you. It could be the scent of your coffee, the scent of fresh air coming in through a window or of a nearby plant. Again, don't judge or analyse, simply experience them.
- If there's food or drink nearby, take a small sip or bite. If there isn't, just become aware of the taste in your mouth. Is it sweet, sour, bitter or something else? Simply note the flavours.
- Take a moment to integrate all the sensations. Acknowledge all the experiences that are constantly available to you, yet often

go unnoticed.

- Finish the exercise by taking a few deep breaths, feeling grateful for your body and its incredible sensory abilities.

Additional Guidance

- This exercise is best done in an environment where you feel comfortable and won't be interrupted.
- When your mind wanders, and it will, gently guide it back to the sense you're focusing on.
- You don't need to spend an equal amount of time on each sense. You might find you're more drawn to one sense over another, and that's perfectly okay.
- Remember, the goal isn't to judge or analyse what you're experiencing but to take notice and simply appreciate the experience.
- This exercise can be done anywhere, whether you're at home, on a walk or at work. The more you practice the more naturally mindful awareness will come to you.

❊ ❊ ❊

CHAPTER 7: SELF CARE

Now and then we need to hit pause on life's fast-paced treadmill and indulge in something that nourishes our spirit, just for the sheer joy of it. As soon as I opened my eyes that morning I knew exactly where I needed to be that day. I followed my intuition, and by 9.00 am I was sitting on the platform waiting for the 9.10 am train to Cardiff. It was just a short train journey from Cardiff to Barry, and soon I found myself stood next to the seawall over looking the beach. My heart lifted and I thanked my intuition for letting me know what my soul needed that day. As I watched the dogs race across the beach, with the beauty of such overwhelming joy at being free, I thought about a quote I had seen a few weeks before: 'Live like someone left the gate open.' How true.

My previous plans for the day had consisted of work and then worry about getting the work done. I was not passionate about the work I was doing at the time and knew it was important to take time out to spend time doing something I love. Coffee in hand, I was in no rush to head home. I stood there for over two hours, just enjoying feeling the love that dogs share so freely. A dog on a beach is a happy dog indeed. My train journey that morning had an almost urgent feel to it, like my soul was running on half-empty. As I made the return trip I felt light, fulfilled and peaceful. I am so thankful to my intuition, telling me I needed to take time out to focus on self-care, knowing it will always show me what I need when I choose to listen.

In many ways, dogs are the essence of self-care. They instinctively know when they need rest, seek comfort and when it's time to play and let off steam. They listen to their bodies and respond to their needs in a way that we, as humans, often neglect to do. Have you noticed how a dog will find the cosiest spot in the house for a nap when they're tired or how they'll relentlessly pursue a bit of fun when they're full of energy? They take their meals seriously, savouring each bite, and they make time to enjoy the simple pleasures in life. They don't push themselves to the point of exhaustion or ignore their basic needs. This is a gentle reminder for us to prioritise our own well-being and to treat ourselves with kindness. Self-care isn't a luxury to squeeze in when we find a bit of free time but a necessity for living a balanced and fulfilling life. Dogs highlight the importance of listening to our bodies and feelings, acknowledging our needs and responding to them in kind.

Imagine if we could incorporate this level of self-care into our daily lives. What if we took the time to truly enjoy our meals instead of eating in a rush, or allowed ourselves to take a nap when we felt drained? What if we made time to engage in activities that bring us joy or simply relaxed to unwind? Dogs teach us that self-care is intuitive and incredibly effective when practiced regularly. It's not about expensive spa days or extravagant vacations, though those can be nice too. It's about the small acts of kindness we show ourselves every day. It's about tuning in to our needs and taking steps to meet them.

Dogs are the ultimate self-care gurus. They don't overthink it or worry about what others might think. They listen to their bodies and do what feels right for them, without a trace of guilt or self-judgement. Dogs don't make excuses or feel guilty about needing a nap in the middle of the day. If they're tired they'll snooze right where they are without a second thought. They're not worried about appearing lazy or unproductive. They understand instinctively that rest is vital for their well-being, and that's a lesson that we, as humans, often forget. In our fast-paced world we're often caught up in the belief that being busy is a badge of honour, that productivity is the ultimate measure of our worth. We push ourselves to the brink of exhaustion, ignoring our bodies' cries for rest, often feeling guilty for taking a break. But what if we could change that mindset? What if we could adopt our dogs' unapologetic approach to self-care? Imagine giving yourself the permission to rest when you need it, take a break without feeling guilty, to prioritise your own well-being without having to justify it. Imagine yourself embracing those moments of relaxation and rejuvenation, guilt-free. Imagine saying no to overwork and yes to a well-balanced life, where rest and relaxation are given the importance they deserve. Think of the positive impact it would have on our mental and physical health. Reduced stress levels, increased productivity, improved mood and overall happiness. These are just a few of the benefits we would enjoy. So, next time you see your dog curled up in the middle of the room, take it as a reminder to take care of yourself unapologetically, knowing it's not just a luxury but an essential aspect of your well-being.

When we adopt the same approach to rest as dogs do, we acknowledge and respect our body's need for downtime. We shed the guilt associated with rest and start seeing it as an essential, not a luxury. Taking cues from dogs we can learn to create our own cosy comfortable spaces where we can unwind, both mentally and physically. By tuning into our bodies, understanding our limits and giving ourselves permission to rest without guilt, we foster a deeper connection with ourselves. This conscious act of self-care not only enhances our overall well-being but also boosts our productivity and creativity in the long run. Just like we watch our dogs curl up for a nap, we're reminded that it's not just okay to rest, it's absolutely necessary.

Ever watched a dog chase after a ball? It's pure joy in motion. Play and movement are not just hobbies for dogs but an essential part of life. A simple game of fetch or a leisurely stroll around the park is more than merely exercise for them, it's a fun-filled celebration of physicality, cognitive stimulation, socialising and overall happiness. There's so much going on in a dog's mind when you throw a ball. The thrill of anticipation, the exhilaration of the chase, the triumph of retrieving the ball and the pride in bringing it back to you. All of this from a single game of fetch. Dogs don't look at these activities as a 'task' or 'exercise'. They're not huffing and puffing thinking, *Phew, got to get my daily cardio in.* No, they're just having great fun. They're playing and loving it and, in doing so, taking care of their bodies and minds. Isn't that a refreshing take on self-care?

What if we were to take a leaf out of our dog's playbook and find joy in physical activities, seeing them not as chores but as fun and enjoyable parts of our day? How might that change our perspective on exercise and self-care? The importance of regular exercise and engaging in activities that bring us joy cannot be overstated. Just like dogs, physical activity for us humans can significantly enhance our cardiovascular health, boost our mood, help us manage stress and improve our overall mental well-being. Choosing activities that we genuinely enjoy, whether it's dancing, walking, practicing yoga or playing a sport, increases the likelihood of consistency. When we genuinely enjoy what we're doing, exercise becomes something we eagerly look forward to, rather than a dreaded task on our to-do list.

Have you ever noticed how much time dogs spend grooming themselves? They meticulously groom their fur, keep it free from dirt and lick their wounds to keep them clean. They groom each other in their pack, all the while bonding while being productive. This isn't just a survival tactic, it's an integral part of their overall well-being. Whether they're grooming themselves, or being groomed by their human companions, it's typically a soothing and enjoyable experience for them. You can often see a dog close its eyes and relax into the process, displaying clear contentment.
This dedication to cleanliness can really give us humans something to think about. Regular bathing, oral hygiene and taking care of our hair and skin are not just about looking good; they are critical for our health, helping to prevent diseases and infections. They also do wonders for our mental well-being and

self-esteem. Looking good means feeling good and presenting a confident self to the world. Just imagine transforming your daily grooming rituals into a mindful, relaxing self-care practice. Picture sinking into a warm bath at the end of a long day, soaking away all your stress, or taking the time for a skincare routine, slowing down and focusing on your well-being as you nourish your skin. Doesn't that sound like something you'd look forward to? How can you make your personal grooming practices more mindful and enjoyable, transforming them into self-care rituals that enhance your overall well-being?

Dogs have it all figured out. They remind us that self-care isn't about fancy spas or expensive retreats; it's about listening to what we need, right here and now and that it's okay to take a nap, enjoy a run or have a good grooming session. They're self-care pros. The exercises at the end of this chapter are your way to join the 'Self-Care Dog Club'. Remember, just like your dog doesn't compromise on its well-being, you shouldn't either. Life's too short not to pamper yourself.

* * *

Exercise 1: Nap Time. Refresh and Recharge.

This exercise is designed to guide you through the process of incorporating restful breaks or naps into your daily routine to help you rejuvenate and enhance your overall well-being. Regular naps can offer many benefits such as improved mood, increased alertness and reduced fatigue. It's like giving yourself a mini-refresh during the day.

Instructions

- Find a cosy peaceful spot where you can comfortably lie down. It can be a favourite chair, a cushioned corner of your couch or your bed. Ensure the environment is quiet and free from distractions.

- Make the area inviting and conducive to relaxation. Arrange pillows or cushions to support your body and create a comfortable position. Consider dimming the lights or using a sleep mask to create a more serene atmosphere.
- Before settling into your chosen spot disconnect from electronic devices and put them away. Silence notifications on your phone or set it to 'Do Not Disturb' mode. This will help create an uninterrupted space for rest and rejuvenation.
- Determine how long you'd like to dedicate to your nap. It can range from a quick power nap of ten to twenty minutes to a longer session of sixty to ninety minutes.
- Before lying down, engage in a brief relaxation ritual to calm your mind and body. Take a few slow, deep breaths, allowing the tension to melt away with each exhale. Scan your body from head to toe consciously, releasing any areas of tension or tightness.
- Once relaxed, settle into your chosen position, ensuring your body feels supported and at ease. You may choose to lie on your back, your side or adopt any position that feels comfortable for you. Adjust the pillows or cushions as needed to find the ideal position.
- Allow yourself to surrender to the peacefulness of the moment. Close your eyes and let go of any thoughts or worries. Focus on your breath, allowing it to flow naturally. If your mind wanders gently bring your attention back to the sensation of your breath.
- After the allotted time has passed gradually bring yourself back to awareness. Stretch your body gently, giving yourself a moment to transition from the restful state to a wakeful one. Take your time and avoid rushing back into your activities.

Additional Guidance

- Choose a nap duration that works best for you, considering your energy levels and the time you have available. Short power naps can provide a quick burst of rejuvenation, while longer naps can help address accumulated fatigue.

- Experiment with different relaxation techniques to enhance your nap experience such as playing calming music, using aromatherapy or practicing progressive muscle relaxation before settling into your nap.
- Ensure that the space where you nap is at a comfortable temperature, neither too warm nor too cold, to promote a restful sleep environment.
- Be consistent with your nap routine to establish a pattern and train your body to recognise the designated time for rest. This can lead to more effective and refreshing naps over time.
- Avoid napping too close to your bedtime, as it may interfere with your regular sleep schedule. Find a balance that allows you to recharge without disrupting your night time sleep.
- If you struggle with falling asleep during naps focus instead on quieting your mind and allowing your body to enter a state of deep relaxation. Even if you don't fall asleep, the restful break can still rejuvenate your energy levels.

Exercise 2: Cleansing Ritual.

This exercise is all about adopting a mindful and intentional approach to your personal care routine, turning it into a holistic self-care practice. By engaging in this self-care ritual inspired by dogs' instinctual self-care practices, you honour your body, mind and emotions.

Instructions

- Find a well-lit comfortable space where you can focus on your cleansing ritual. Ensure the area is organised, creating a soothing atmosphere for your self-care practice.
- Allow yourself enough time to engage in the whole process without rushing. This will ensure you can fully immerse yourself in the experience and enjoy its benefits.

- Gather all the tools you will need. This may include a brush or comb for your hair, skincare products, a mirror and any other items specific to your needs. Having everything ready will streamline the process and minimise distractions.
- Before you begin take a moment to centre yourself. Take a few deep breaths, allowing your body and mind to relax. This intentional pause helps shift your focus to the present moment and prepares you for the self-care experience ahead.
- Begin by caring for your hair. Brush or comb it gently, removing any tangles or knots with care. Notice the sensation of the brush or comb on your scalp, tuning into the physical experience as you tend to your hair.
- Move on to your skincare routine if applicable. Cleanse your face with a gentle cleanser, using circular motions to massage your skin. Apply moisturizer or any other skincare products that are part of your routine. As you do so, pay attention to the sensations, scents and textures, fully engaging your senses in the process.
- Take a moment to look at yourself in the mirror. Gaze into your own eyes, acknowledging your unique beauty and worth. Offer yourself words of kindness and affirmation, reinforcing a positive self-image. Allow yourself to connect with your inner self, fostering self-compassion and acceptance.
- Continue with your personal grooming routine such as trimming nails, styling your hair or carrying out other self-care practices that contribute to your well-being. Take your time and be gentle with yourself, approaching each step with mindfulness and self-love.
- As you complete your ritual express, gratitude for the opportunity to care for yourself. Take a moment to appreciate your body, its resilience and the efforts you invest in your well-being. Cultivate a sense of gratitude for the self-care practice you've just engaged in.
- After completing the self-care ritual, carry the positive energy and mindset with you throughout the day. Allow the experience to remind you of your worth and the importance of nurturing

yourself regularly.

Additional Guidance

- Customize the self-care ritual according to your personal preferences and needs. Adapt the steps to align with your routine and incorporate any additional practices that promote self-care for you.
- Engage your senses fully during the process. Pay attention to the smells, textures and sensations involved, allowing yourself to be fully present in the moment.
- Treat this ritual as a sacred time dedicated to yourself. Avoid distractions such as phone calls, emails or social media notifications that can disrupt your focus and detract from the self-care experience.
- Explore the possibility of incorporating soothing music or aromatherapy into your ritual to enhance relaxation and create a spa-like ambiance.
- Remember, this ritual isn't just about physical grooming; it's about nurturing your emotional well-being. Use this time to practice self-compassion and self-love, embracing the holistic nature of self-care.
- Be gentle and patient with yourself throughout the grooming ritual. Treat your body with care and kindness, recognising that this is a form of self-nurturing and a reflection of your self-worth.
- Consider turning your grooming ritual into a sensory experience. Use scented products that evoke positive emotions or play calming music in the background. Engaging multiple senses can enhance the soothing and rejuvenating effects of the ritual.
- Embrace a mindful approach by focusing on each step and immerse yourself fully in the present moment. Notice the sensations, thoughts and emotions that arise during the process, acknowledging them without judgement.
- Remember, this exercise isn't solely about outward appearance but also about cultivating a positive relationship with yourself. Use the mirror reflection step as an opportunity to connect with

your inner self, appreciating your unique qualities and expressing gratitude for your body and mind.

Exercise 3: Cultivating Healthy Boundaries

Putting personal boundaries in place is an essential part of self-care that encourages you to define your limits, express them to others and protect your emotional well-being. When boundaries are unclear or violated we often end up feeling overwhelmed, drained or resentful. That's where this exercise can be useful. By engaging in this exercise you cultivate a sense of self-respect and protect your emotional well-being. Remember, like dogs instinctively protect their personal space, you can protect your emotional energy and environment.

Instructions

- Take some time for self-reflection to gain clarity about your needs, values and personal limits. Reflect on the areas of your life where you feel overwhelmed, resentful or drained. Identify situations where setting boundaries would benefit your emotional well-being.
- Determine the boundaries you wish to set in different areas of your life, such as relationships, work and personal time. Consider what behaviours, requests or situations are crossing your boundaries and causing discomfort. Make clear what is acceptable and what is not based on your self-reflection.
- Practice assertive communication by clearly and respectfully expressing your boundaries to others. Choose an appropriate time and place to have a conversation and use 'I' statements to express how you feel and what you need. Be firm and direct in stating your boundaries, emphasising the importance of self-care and emotional well-being.
- Practice saying no when your boundaries are being crossed or when you need to prioritise your own needs. Saying no is not a selfish act but a way to honour and protect your emotional well-

being. Be firm but polite and avoid over-explaining or justifying your decision.

- Implement boundaries in your daily life to cultivate balance and protect your emotional energy. This may include setting limits on the time and energy you allocate to work, social engagements or personal commitments. Respect your boundaries by scheduling self-care activities and downtime to recharge.
- Pay attention to how others respond to your boundaries. Some may respect and appreciate your self-care efforts while others may push against them. Observe any reactions or pushback and remain firm in maintaining your boundaries. Evaluate and adjust your boundaries as needed to find the right balance for your emotional well-being.
- Be kind to yourself throughout this process. It takes time to establish and maintain healthy boundaries. Understand that setting boundaries is an ongoing practice and it's natural to encounter challenges along the way. Practice self-compassion and remain flexible in adjusting boundaries when necessary.
- If you find it challenging to set or maintain boundaries, seek support from trusted friends, family or professionals such as therapists or coaches. They can provide guidance, encouragement and insights to help you navigate this journey of boundary setting.

Additional Guidance

- Start with small boundaries and gradually expand to larger ones. Building confidence in setting boundaries takes practice.
- Remember that setting boundaries is not about controlling others but about taking responsibility for your own well-being.
- Be aware of any guilt or discomfort that may arise when setting boundaries. It's normal to experience these emotions, but don't let them deter you from prioritising your emotional health.
- Practice active listening and empathy when others express their boundaries to you. Respect their limits just as you expect others to respect yours.

- Regularly reassess and adjust your boundaries as your needs and circumstances change. Flexibility is key to maintaining healthy boundaries in different situations.

* * *

CHAPTER 8: PLAY

The trip to the seaside had been planned for weeks. I opened the curtains, viewed the ominous grey clouds and considered postponing. The weather was certainly not your, 'hey, let's visit the beach today,' sort of day. It was overcast, and there was a hint of rain in the air. I heard my mobile ring and immediately knew who it would be on the other end.

'Have you left yet? We need to make an early start. I am so excited!'

Postpone? Who was I trying to kid? I smiled and quietly sighed, trying to remember where I had put my light raincoat. Soon we were on our way to Ogmore-on-Sea, a beautiful small town on the coast in South Wales. Even though the weather was dull, the atmosphere inside the car was full of sunshine. Lucy was born in Wales and loved the sea. She loved her dog even more. From the day she collected Harvey as a tiny bundle of fluff they were inseparable. The loyalty dogs show is limitless, and Harvey was no exception. He had been Lucy's shadow through years of difficulties. The thought of that little dog had kept her fighting to survive the torment that she battled throughout her life.

We arrived and scrambled down onto the secluded beach. Harvey was beside himself with excitement, running round madly in circles digging frantically in the sand looking for buried treasure. Lucy's face was already red from the wind and cold, but as she turned to me and smiled. I knew that nothing mattered other than enjoying this moment. The beach was ours that day; we did not see a single other person. One hundred? Two hundred? I lost count of the number of times we threw the ball into the sea for Harvey. Each time he went bounding into the waves with as much excitement as the first time, proudly retrieving the ball and dropping it back at our feet. Again, again. Come on, throw it in! After a while we had to stop as he was shivering with cold, but his little face shown the determination to carry on regardless. It was with reluctance that we left the beach and went back to the car to get warm.

By this time the rain had arrived. We were soggy, windswept and cold but felt incredibly happy. It was a few hours of freedom. The expanse of sand and the pounding of the waves bringing to light the healing power of nature. The journey home was quiet. Harvey fell asleep almost instantly, and as I listened to his gentle contented snores, I felt grateful that I had not postponed our trip that day. I glanced over at Lucy. She had her eyes shut and the most beautiful smile lit up her face. Seeing my bestie happy and the sound and smell of the sea had done an amazing job of sweeping away all my worries. As I turned my attention back to the road for the journey home, I smiled and said a silent thank you for the people in my life and the memories we share.

I can still picture Harvey's eyes now, shining with joy, tail wagging like mad, the moment he anticipated the ball being thrown into the sea. That pure happiness they find in play is infectious, isn't it? The wonderful thing about dogs is how they seize the day. Rain or shine, they're always ready for fun. See a leaf fluttering in the breeze? It's a new toy, their whole world becomes that leaf. They're all consumed in that moment with no second thoughts or distractions. What they're really showing us is how to live in the present, how to let go and how to find joy in the simple unexpected moments of life. When was the last time you truly lived in the moment like that, when you let go of past regrets and future anxieties and just basked in the moment?

We often get caught up in the rat race and overlook the small pleasures that life offers. But dogs? They've got this figured out. Have you seen a dog chasing its tail or playing fetch? There's no prize at the end, just the pure unadulterated joy of the game itself. They take pleasure in these simple moments and in doing so remind us to find joy in our own everyday experiences. Just as dogs delight in a game of fetch or a leisurely walk in the park, we, too, can discover joy in our everyday experiences. Turn up the music that makes your heart sing and let your body move freely, dance as if you're the only person in the world. These ordinary moments can offer unexpected joy and upliftment. What simple joys do you overlook in the hustle and bustle of life?

Dogs are masters of authenticity. When they play they're not worried about looking silly or fitting in. They're not concerned about being judged or appearing too excited. They're entirely wrapped up in the thrill of the moment, completely uninhibited in their happiness. They wag their tails with abandon, bark with pure delight and jump about without a shred of self-consciousness. It's as if they're saying, 'This is me, and I'm loving every moment of life!' They don't filter their joy or dampen their enthusiasm to suit the world around them. Their expressions are honest and unguarded, a true reflection of their inner selves.

Isn't that such a refreshing approach? Can you imagine living with that level of freedom, being true to yourself without the fear of being judged or the need for approval? How liberating would it be to express ourselves fully, to let go of our inhibitions, to live life on our own terms, just like dogs do? What if we could apply this to our own lives? What if we could throw off the restraints of social expectations and express ourselves authentically? Would we laugh louder, dance more freely, love more openly and live more fully? How many of our choices are influenced by what we think others might think? What if we could make those choices based on what truly brings us joy? Imagine the changes that could occur in our lives. Embrace the freedom that comes with uninhibited expression, just like dogs do, and watch as your life flourishes in the most lovely ways.

Dogs offer us a valuable lesson about the magic of play in our own relationships. Their desire for play doesn't just keep them active and happy; it also fosters deep bonds of trust, companionship and mutual understanding. Dogs don't play games to win; they play for the sheer fun of it, for the enjoyment of shared activity and mutual interaction. Think about the laughter, light-heartedness and the joy that comes with these moments. Have you noticed how it breaks down barriers, opens up communication and creates a shared sense of enjoyment? There's an instant connection, a bonding experience that's born out of these playful moments. What if we could bring the same spirit of playfulness into our interactions with our family, friends, colleagues or even our neighbours? What if we made time for shared jokes, spontaneous games or just simple fun activities that bring us together in shared enjoyment? It's these moments of joy, laughter and play that create lasting memories and foster a sense of camaraderie. It's where connections are strengthened and bonds are deepened. Incorporating more play into our relationships, like dogs do, could not only bring more joy into our lives but also foster a sense of community, belonging and mutual understanding. It's about making time to enjoy each other's company, laugh together and create shared experiences.

In the dog's world, playtime is not just for amusement but a stress therapy, an energy outlet and a source of enduring joy. Whether they're chasing a ball, playing with a fellow dog or simply running around with lively abandon, dogs incorporate play as a crucial part of their daily lives. Their behaviour provides an ideal escape from stress and boredom, unleashing a torrent of pent-up energy, infusing their lives with a lively sense of joy. They bring an enthusiastic curiosity to their play, exploring their surroundings with an insatiable interest, hunting for new scents and adopting new 'toys' in their environment. It's as though every day brings a new adventure and a new opportunity for play, which they seize with enthusiasm. Adopting this dog-inspired attitude can revolutionise our approach to stress and personal growth. What if we approached our everyday experiences with a renewed sense of curiosity and the spirit of play? Could we transform routine tasks into playful exploration? Could we infuse our lives with the adventurous spirit of a dog at play?

Play isn't just a pastime for dogs; it's a way of life. It's not just about having fun; it's about being present, expressing themselves authentically, strengthening relationships and letting off steam. We can bring all that goodness into our own lives by embracing the spirit of play. Understanding all this is just the beginning. The real magic happens when you put it into practice and that's why the exercises at the end of this chapter are so important. They're designed to help you apply these lessons to your life and emphasise the value of play. They're your chance to bring out that playful spirit and let it shine. Let's take our cue from dogs by shaking off inhibitions to embrace the world with playful enthusiasm. After all, life's too short to miss out on the fun. Let's play!

❊ ❊ ❊

Exercise 1: Playful Pets

This exercise offers an opportunity to bond with dogs, experience shared joy and learn valuable lessons about living in the moment. It's about creating an atmosphere of joy, connection and mutual respect, all while having a fun and playful experience. It encourages us to live in the moment and be fully present.

Instructions

- Find an opportunity to spend time with playful dogs. If you don't have a dog of your own, consider volunteering at an animal shelter or reaching out to friends or family who have dogs and will let you interact with them.

- Create a safe and comfortable environment for both you and the dogs. Ensure there are no potential hazards or distractions that could interrupt your playtime.
- Engage in interactive games that encourage playfulness and create a bond. Common games include fetch, tug-of-war, hide-and-seek or using puzzle toys to challenge their problem-solving skills. Use toys or treats that they enjoy.
- Begin by introducing yourself to the dogs calmly and gently. Allow them to sniff and investigate you, gradually building trust and familiarity. Respect their boundaries and body language. If they seem hesitant or uncomfortable, give them space and time to adjust.
- Once they are comfortable with your presence, start the chosen game or activity. Use positive reinforcement such as treats or verbal praise to reward them for participating. Maintain a playful and enthusiastic tone as dogs respond well to high energy and excitement.
- Observe the dogs' behaviour and adapt your play style accordingly. Some may prefer gentle and interactive play, while others may enjoy more vigorous activities. Pay attention to their cues and adjust your approach to ensure their comfort and enjoyment.
- Interact using a variety of movements and gestures such as throwing a toy for them to fetch, engaging in a gentle tug-of-war or hiding treats around the room for them to find. Allow their natural instincts to guide the play, encouraging their curiosity and exploration.
- Take breaks during play sessions to allow them to rest and recharge. Provide fresh water and ensure they have a comfortable resting area available. Respect their need for breaks and don't overwhelm them with continuous play.
- Remember to enjoy the process and embrace the light-heartedness that comes with play. Laugh, engage in affectionate gestures like petting or belly rubs and create a positive and joyful atmosphere.
- After the play session, spend a few moments observing the

dogs as they wind down. Notice any changes in their behaviour or demeanour as play often leaves them feeling satisfied and content.

Additional Guidance

- Always prioritise the safety and well-being of both yourself and the dogs involved.
- Observe and respect the dogs' boundaries and body language.
- Use positive reinforcement to reward desired behaviour during play.
- Be mindful of any allergies or sensitivities you may have.

Exercise 2: Playful Cooking

This exercise makes cooking a more enjoyable and fulfilling activity. It's about discovering the joy and satisfaction that can come from the creativity and experimentation in the kitchen, turning an everyday task into a source of pleasure, growth and connection. Instead of viewing cooking as a chore or a means to an end, this exercise encourages us to view the kitchen as a playground, a place where we can experiment with flavours, techniques and presentation while also enjoying the process and end results.

Instructions

- Set aside dedicated time in your schedule to engage in playful cooking. Choose a day or evening when you have plenty of time and a relaxed mindset to fully engage in the experience.
- Explore new recipes or ingredients that excite you. Look for unique flavour combinations, innovative cooking techniques or dishes from different cuisines.
- Make a list of the ingredients you'll need, and gather them before you begin. Having everything readily available will ensure a smooth and enjoyable cooking process.
- Create a playful atmosphere in your kitchen. Put on some

lively music, wear a chef's hat or apron and set out colourful cooking utensils or quirky kitchen gadgets. Embrace the fun and creativity that cooking can offer.

- Approach the recipes with a spirit of playfulness and curiosity. Feel free to deviate from the instructions, tweak the ingredients or add your own personal touch. Allow your imagination to guide you as you experiment and explore.
- Embrace new flavour combinations by adding herbs, spices or seasonings that you may not have used before. Be open to the unexpected and trust your taste buds to guide you.
- Get creative with the presentation of your creations. Experiment with plating techniques, garnishes and food styling. Let your artistic side shine as you transform your dishes into visually appealing masterpieces.
- Once you've finished cooking, take a moment to savour and enjoy your creations. Sit down and fully immerse yourself in the flavours, textures and aromas of your playful dishes. Appreciate the effort and creativity you put into each bite.
- Share your delicious creations with others. Invite friends, family or neighbours to join you for a playful cooking showcase, or organise a potluck where everyone can share their cookery experiments. Embrace the joy of cooking as a social activity that brings people together.

Additional Guidance

- Don't be afraid to make mistakes. Playful cooking is all about embracing the process and learning from each experience.
- Embrace the journey rather than focusing solely on the end result. The joy lies in the exploration and experimentation.
- Take photos of your creations to capture the memories and inspire future cookery adventures.
- Keep a journal or recipe book to record your favourite recipes and ideas for future reference.
- Embrace the opportunity to expand your palate and discover new flavours and ingredients.

- Remember, playful cooking is about embracing your creativity, experimenting with flavours and having fun in the kitchen. By approaching cooking with a light-hearted and curious mindset, you can unlock a world of cookery delights and share the joy of your creations with others.

Exercise 3: Playful Sports

This exercise is designed to introduce the concept of play into sports and recreational activities, with the aim of adopting enjoyment, curiosity, social interaction and personal growth. Often, sports are viewed through a competitive lens where winning is the main aim. This exercise encourages us to approach sports with a playful mindset, emphasising the joy of participation, learning and improvement over the necessity of winning or achieving specific goals. It's about finding joy in the process, celebrating personal achievements, promoting physical activity and fostering connections with others, all while having a lot of fun along the way.

Instructions

- Identify a range of sports or recreational activities that grab your interest. Consider both traditional sports and unique activities that you've been curious about. Some examples include soccer, basketball, tennis, swimming, yoga or trying out a new dance style.
- Consider factors such as your physical abilities, interests and accessibility to equipment or facilities. Remember, the goal is to engage in activities that bring you joy and a sense of playfulness.
- Start by researching local sports clubs, community centres or recreational facilities where you can take part in these activities. Look for classes, open sessions or events that cater to beginners or those interested in casual play.
- Prepare yourself physically and mentally for the activity. Warm up your body with light stretches or exercises to prevent

injuries and promote flexibility. Mentally, adopt a mindset of curiosity, openness and a willingness to learn and try new things.

- Gather any necessary equipment required for the activity. This may include sports shoes, appropriate clothing, protective gear or any specific equipment needed for the chosen sport. Ensuring you have the right equipment will enhance your enjoyment and safety during play.
- Engage in the chosen sport or activity with a spirit of fun and playfulness. Embrace the joy of movement, challenge yourself to try new skills and focus on enjoying the process rather than achieving specific outcomes. Let go of self-consciousness and fully immerse yourself in the activity.
- Play with others who share your enthusiasm for the sport or activity. Join teams, take part in group classes or invite friends to join you. Playing with others not only adds a social element but also fosters friendly competition, camaraderie and shared experiences.
- Embrace the opportunity to learn from others and seek guidance or advice from more experienced players or instructors. Be open to constructive feedback, as it can help you improve your skills and deepen your understanding of the sport or activity.
- Take breaks during play sessions to rest, hydrate and appreciate the moments of playfulness. Reflect on the joy, laughter and positive energy generated during the sports or recreational activity.

Additional Guidance

- Listen to your body and know your limits. Pace yourself and don't push beyond what feels comfortable or safe for you.
- Focus on the process of play rather than the outcome. Embrace the journey of learning and improvement rather than fixating on winning or achieving specific goals.
- Stay hydrated, wear appropriate protective gear and follow safety guidelines to ensure a safe and enjoyable experience.
- Be respectful of others' boundaries, both physically and

emotionally, during the sports or recreational activity.

- Celebrate your achievements, no matter how small, and acknowledge the effort you put into engaging in playful sports.

* * *

CHAPTER 9: AGING

If someone asked me how I would describe Dave, I would not hesitate in my reply, not having to consider it for a single second. Fun. A big happy grown-up kid, full of wonderful ideas who is convinced anything is possible. Now in his late fifties, he is still as fun loving as ever, showing no signs of slowing down. His child within is definitely awake and in charge. Everyone he meets adores him, and they are so blessed to have someone in their life who has never forgotten the art of how to play.

'I bought a boat.'

'You did what? A boat? Where on earth are you going to put a boat?'

'I've always wanted one. Imagine being able to go out and do some serious sea fishing. I can't wait to tell Darren; he will love it.'

No problem, nothing is impossible, believe and it will happen, things will work out, it will be fun! It transpired that the boat - in my minds' eye fifty feet with a sail - was in fact a ribbed dinghy with an on-board motor.

'It's fine, Nanny, honestly. You will be able to make it down to the beach. It's not a cliff, more like a little steep hill, but Chris and I will help you.'

Nanny, your mum, who was always referred to as Nanny, was in her seventies and not as agile as she used to be, but you were determined that she should always feel as though she had the confidence and ability to tackle anything. If you and the kids were going on a mad scramble, down a steep set of rocks in Cornwall to get the very best fishing spot, then Nanny was going too.

'Honestly love, it will be fine. They will ignore you if you ignore them. This is the perfect spot for a picnic.'

You could not come to my rescue as the swan chased me down the bank, her tail feathers shaking with rage, spitting venom at me, as I dared to get too close to her nest. However, you did manage to come to my rescue once you had picked yourself up off the floor from laughing so much.

'Dave, you are a card, look at you!'

Shelia howled with laughter, tears streaming down her face. Dave was wearing full makeup. After helping her to apply some eyeshadow and lipstick he applied his own. She was one of our favourite clients on the care round, bed bound and poorly, who loved to laugh. She adored him, but then again they all did. Some of the clients did not want a male carer, except Dave of course. He was gentle, respectful, funny and kind. His dream, should he win the lottery, was to open a care home that was a home for kids who happened to be pensioners. It would be filled with fun, games, laughter and kindness, all designed to ease any loneliness or pain. If I do, by any chance, win the lottery, it will be yours.

'I got rid of Jenny and bought this.'

'Got rid of Jenny? But you loved that car.'

'Yes, but I can get a wheelchair in the back of this one so I can take Ben out to all the places he wants to go.'

You were a full-time carer for an older gentleman, and,until you came along, he went to a day centre for one afternoon a week while the rest of the week he simply existed. Soon the whole week was a packed itinerary of things to do, places to visit, people to see.

'I thought you said it was down this road. It's a dead-end Ben.'

You both looked at each other and burst out laughing. It didn't matter. You were out and about, that you were hopelessly lost just added to the fun. I'm not sure who had the most fun, you or him. His family was so grateful.

'Please never leave will you? You have transformed our dad's life. He loves you. We love you. You are amazing.'

You had lost both of your brothers in their mid-thirties, both with children and families who loved them. I think that is why you played so hard and brought so much happiness into the lives of others, knowing how life can be cut short so suddenly, knowing the importance of living for today, never giving a thought to getting older, believing anything is possible.

Let's take a moment to consider an overlooked virtue of dogs, the way they handle aging. Despite the aches and pains, the diminished eyesight or the slower pace, dogs carry themselves with such grace and dignity don't they? Picture an older dog on a walk. Their joints may be stiff and their eyes not as sharp as they used to be, but they still trot along, tails wagging, spirits undeterred. They continue to find joy in their daily routines, their enthusiasm for life seemingly untouched by the years. There's this air of resilience about them, this acceptance of the changes they're going through without any sign of self-pity or despair. This approach towards aging is quite inspiring, don't you think? They don't waste time mourning their lost youth or dwelling on the physical challenges that come with age. Instead, they embrace each new day, each moment, with the same unyielding enthusiasm they had as puppies. They continue to live fully in the present, enjoying the simple pleasures of life and cherishing the love and companionship of their human families.

What if we adopted the same attitude towards our own aging process? Instead of fearing the inevitable changes, what if we embraced them as part of our life's journey? What if we learnt to accept and navigate these changes with the same grace, dignity and positivity as our dogs do? Think about how that could change our perceptions about growing older. Instead of viewing it as something to be dreaded, we could see it as a natural progression of life, an opportunity to grow and develop. We could shift our focus from what we're losing to what we're gaining: wisdom, experience, deeper relationships and a better understanding of ourselves and the world around us.

Dogs teach us a thing or two about paying attention to our bodies and respecting its needs. Whether it's a young pup or an older dog, they have this natural ability to understand what their bodies are telling them and respond accordingly. Have you ever noticed how a dog, when feeling under the weather, will slow down a bit, opting for rest over their usual hyper activities? Or how they seek a quiet, cosy spot when they need some downtime? They don't feel the need to hide their discomfort or to carry on regardless. They listen to their bodies and give it what it needs, whether it's rest, relaxation or a warmer spot in the home, as they instinctively know that the warmth is good for their aging joints.

We need to tune in to what our bodies are telling us, understand the signals they're sending us, and respond in kind. Instead of ignoring our tiredness and pushing ourselves to the point of exhaustion, what if we rested when our bodies are crying out for it? Or, if we're in discomfort, instead of masking it with painkillers what if we sought comfort and treatment? What if we paid more attention to our diet, nourishing our bodies with the right foods, respected our limitations and didn't push ourselves beyond our physical capacity, especially as we get older? By listening to our bodies, by respecting our needs, we could improve our overall health and wellbeing. It's not about giving in to every little ache and pain. It's about understanding and responding to our bodies' needs. It's about practicing self-care like dogs do so well.

Dogs wear their greying fur as a badge of honour, a testament to all the life experiences they've gathered over the years. Their eyes maybe a touch cloudier than in their puppy days, but they brim over with wisdom and understanding. It's as if they've seen it all and made peace with it. Have you ever really looked into the eyes of an aging dog? There's a serene acceptance there, an understanding that's hard to put into words. It's like they've figured out the secret to aging, embraced it as another part of the journey, not as something to be feared or resisted. Isn't that an amazing outlook to have? Imagine how different our own perspective on aging could be if we took a leaf out of our dogs' book. Instead of dreading the inevitable we could simply accept it, adapt to our changing circumstances and embrace our new reality.

Dogs are the perfect example of the beauty in aging. They don't dread it or try to ward it off with lotions and potions but take it in their stride, accepting it as an inevitable and natural part of life. It's as if they've unlocked the secret that we humans often struggle to grasp: that aging isn't a period of decline but another chapter, filled with its own unique experiences and joys. Can you imagine if we adopted a dog's attitude towards aging? How liberating would it be to view our wrinkles and see them as something to be proud of? They're like a road map of our life, a testament to our journey, each line representing a story, a memory, an experience that shaped us. What if we viewed our bodies not with criticism or disappointment but instead with deep respect and admiration for how far they've come, how much they've endured? After all, these bodies of ours have been our vessels, carrying us through life's highs and lows. The next time those worries about growing old creep in take a moment to observe your dog. Take note of the greying fur, the wisdom in their eyes and their spirit that remains undimmed despite their advancing years. Let them be your guide and inspiration to age with grace, dignity and acceptance. Let's not forget that aging is not a burden but a privilege, one that not everyone is lucky enough to experience. Isn't it more fulfilling to grow old with grace than to resist the natural flow of life?

One quality of dogs that's often striking, particularly as they age, is their adaptability. They may not jump as high as they once could and their zoomies may have slowed down, but they don't let these changes reduce their joy. They simply adapt and get on with life with their typical resilience and unflinching adaptability. How often do we humans resist change? It's almost as if we've been programmed to fear it, especially when it comes to aging. The mere thought of losing our youthfulness or having to contend with a changing body often sends us into a whirl of worry and anxiety, but these fears are rooted in our inability to accept change as a natural part of life's cycle. Now, take a leaf out of a dog's life. They age like we do. Their bodies change and they may lose some of their youthful flexibility. But, unlike us, they don't worry about this change or resist it. Instead, they accept it, adapt to it and continue to find joy in life. It's as if they're telling us that change isn't something to be feared but embraced. So, what if we applied this dog's wisdom to our own lives? What if we saw aging not as a process to be feared but as an opportunity to adapt and grow? What if we took these changes in our stride, found new ways to enjoy life, and continued to live with the same passion as in our youth? Adapting to change, rather than resisting it, could help ease our anxieties about aging and allow us to appreciate each stage of our life's journey.

Through their resilience, adaptability and grace, dogs paint a picture of aging that is far removed from the fears and anxieties we often hold. Their lives may be shorter but dogs grasp something about aging that we humans sometimes cannot accept. Age isn't only about aches and pains, greying hairs or slowing bodies but about resilience, understanding our bodies and adjusting to change rather than resisting it. Dogs show us the beauty of growing older, the dignity in aging and the wisdom that comes with passing years. If we can embrace these lessons and apply them to our lives, we might find ourselves less afraid of the ticking clock and more ready to embrace the joys and wisdom that each new day brings. The next time you see an older dog, wagging its tail and joyfully embracing life despite the challenges of age, let it serve as a reminder to approach your own aging process with the same resilience, grace and positivity.

Try the following exercises. They are designed not only to help you understand the lessons in this chapter but to enable you to apply them in your life. They will guide you to reflect and ultimately transform your perception of aging and health, because if we can learn to age as gracefully as dogs, if we can keep our youthful spirit alive even as we grow older, we would have discovered that, no matter how many years pass by, we can still chase our dreams and live each day with the grace and dignity that dogs demonstrate so beautifully.

* * *

Exercise 1: Daily Reflection on Change

This exercise cultivates an acceptance of change as a natural part of life. It encourages mindfulness and presence, allowing you to witness life's constant flow without fear or resistance, and helps you become more attuned to life's constant change, promoting acceptance and peace in the face of the inevitable.

Instructions

- At the end of your day, find a peaceful spot where you can sit undisturbed for a few minutes. Make sure this is a place where you feel comfortable and at ease.
- Before you start, take a few deep breaths to calm your mind.

Breathe in slowly through your nose, hold your breath for a few seconds and exhale through your mouth. Repeat this a few times until you feel your body relax and your mind quieten.

- Think back over your day, from the moment you woke up through to the present moment. Reflect on the events, interactions, feelings and thoughts you experienced.
- As you think back, identify elements of your day that represent change. These can be physical changes, like a haircut, or a new item in your home. It can be changes in your environment, like a shift in weather or a new route to work. It could also be internal changes, like a shift in your mood or perspective.
- Acknowledge each change you identify without judgement. Try not to label these changes as 'good' or 'bad'. Instead, see them as neutral events, a natural part of life's ebb and flow.
- You might find it helpful to write your observations in a journal. This can serve as a record of your progress and a visible reflection of life's ever-changing nature.

Additional Guidance

- Be patient with yourself. This exercise is about observation and acceptance, not critique or judgement.
- Remember, there's no 'right' or 'wrong' in this exercise. The aim is to note changes, big or small, not to assess their value or worth.
- This practice is not about generating change but acknowledging it. You are not expected to create change; instead, you're learning to recognise and accept it.
- If you find it difficult to identify changes, start with something simple like the change of day into night or the shift in temperature.
- With regular practice you will find yourself becoming more resilient in the face of change.

Exercise 2: Aging Gracefully Visualisation

This exercise fosters a positive, accepting and graceful outlook on aging. It encourages you to envision your future self in a positive light rather than with fear or apprehension. Visualisation is a powerful tool that can help shape our perception of reality, and in this case, it will help in transforming our views on aging. Aging is a natural process, and this exercise is meant to help us view it with grace, acceptance and joy.

Instructions

- Find a quiet relaxing spot where you won't be disturbed. You may choose to dim the lights or play some soft, soothing music to help create a peaceful atmosphere.
- Sit comfortably, close your eyes and take a few deep breaths. As you breathe in, feel your body fill with calm, and as you breathe out, let go of any tension or stress. Continue this process until you feel your body fully relaxed.
- Begin by visualising yourself as you are now. Notice your appearance, health, emotions and environment. Try to picture this as vividly as possible.
- Now, imagine time flowing forward, like the pages of a calendar flipping in the wind. Visualise the seasons changing, birthdays passing and your surroundings transforming over time.
- As time flows forward in your mind, visualise your future older self. See your hair greying, skin showing signs of age and your body changing with time. Remember, these changes are natural and inevitable.
- Picture your older self with a smile, filled with joy and wisdom. Visualise yourself aging gracefully, living each day with enthusiasm and contentment. Embody the dignity and resilience that dogs show as they age.
- Spend a few moments holding this vision in your mind, truly embracing the image of your graceful, aging self. Let this image fill you with a sense of peace and acceptance.

- Once you have completed your visualisation jot down a few notes about the experience in your journal. What did you notice? How did you feel? This can help reinforce the experience and track your progress over time.

Additional Guidance

- Visualisation works best when it's specific and detailed. Try to include as many details as possible.
- It's normal for your mind to wander. If it does, gently guide your focus back to your visualisation.
- Remember, this is a positive visualisation. If negative thoughts or fears arise acknowledge them and let them go, returning your focus to the positive vision of your future self.
- If you're having difficulty creating a mental image don't worry. Everyone visualises differently. Some people may see clear, vivid images, while others might have a more abstract sense. What's important is the feeling and intent behind the visualisation, not the clarity of the mental image.

Exercise 3: Embracing Your Looks

The aim of this exercise is to choose self-love and acceptance, particularly regarding our physical appearance and the changes it undergoes as we age. It encourages us to view these changes not as flaws but as signs of wisdom, experience and the beautiful journey of life. Like dogs, who don't fuss over their appearances, we need to learn to love and embrace our looks. Through this exercise, we can learn to love our reflection in the mirror, not despite the signs of aging, but because of them.

Instructions:

- This exercise requires a mirror, ideally full length, but if that's not available any mirror where you can clearly see yourself will work.

- Stand in front of the mirror with your body relaxed and your posture erect. Breathe deeply and centre yourself.
- Spend a moment taking in your reflection. Look at your face, body and posture. Notice the details, the colour of your eyes, shape of your lips, lines of your face and the build of your body.
- As you look at your reflection, consciously note the changes your body has undergone over time. This could be grey hair, wrinkles, a change in body shape, anything that stands out as a sign of aging.
- Now, give yourself a genuine compliment. This could relate to a body part, 'My eyes are really beautiful,' or your aging signs as marks of wisdom and experience, 'These laugh lines show all the joy I've experienced in my life.'
- Embrace your aging appearance with acceptance and grace, understanding that they are a natural part of life's journey and each sign of aging is a testament to your lived experiences.
- Repeat this exercise daily. Over time it can significantly improve your self-esteem and acceptance of your aging self.

Additional Guidance

- It's essential that the compliments you give yourself are genuine. You need to believe them for the exercise to have a lasting impact.
- If you find it challenging to compliment yourself start with something simple and build up from there.
- If negative thoughts arise during this exercise, acknowledge them without judgement and return to the task at hand. The aim is to focus on the positive.
- Consider keeping a journal to record the compliments you give yourself. Over time, reviewing this journal can serve as a reminder to practice self-love and acceptance.

CHAPTER 10: RESILIENCE

Masie seemed extra loving since I had become pregnant, nesting up close to the baby bump protectively. I had to rest when I got the chance, as I was thirty eight weeks pregnant and still working, not being able to afford to have too much time off. My baby's dad was busy having a relationship with someone else during my pregnancy, something I found out a few months later. He was emotionally abusive, and I dared not question where the money went each month. We never had enough money to pay all the bills and to buy the items we needed for the new arrival.

It was two days until the end of the month. I dared to look in my purse. Fifty-five pence. Food banks were not in place thirty years ago, so I had the choice of buying a tin of dog food or a loaf of bread. Maise was duly fed, and I got through until pay day. As I sat and considered my future, I knew I could not find myself in a position like this again. I needed to change my life, improve my prospects and earn enough to provide for my baby. I did not realise that this day would motivate me to sign up for further education and, subsequently, open doors to some amazing opportunities, resulting in me achieving dreams today I would never have thought possible all those years ago.

I studied whenever I could. Being a single mum with a part-time job whilst trying to complete a degree was tough but I dug in and resilience got me through alongside support from my amazing mum and wonderful friends. Grandmother and Grandson grew incredibly close because of the time she spent looking after him. They still share a special bond today. 'I am so proud of my boy,' I would say.

'No, he's *our* boy,' she would insist.

I smiled and could only agree. Sam's childhood was cloaked in the love of my mum and his step-mum they showered upon him. Two of the most wonderful and caring women in the world. Today he is a group counsellor, there for all his friends in their time of need, always ready to help and listen. He was trained by the best.

Sometimes, somehow, we need to find the strength and resilience to get through life's challenging times, and dogs can teach us some valuable lessons in the art of doing this. Resilience is to persist and maintain a sense of hope, even when times are hard. It's an enduring spirit that weathers all storms, not because it is immune to hardship, but because it refuses to be overwhelmed by it. Imagine a tree that bends but doesn't break in a storm. That's resilience. It's about flexibility in the face of adversity. It's not about standing rigid and unyielding, because that can lead to snapping or breaking. Instead, it's about learning to sway with the winds of change, bend a little, adjust our sails if we are to weather the storm, and then stand tall again when the storm passes. Ultimately, resilience is about the courage to keep going, the flexibility to adapt, the strength to endure and to keep hope alive. It's a trait that we all can cultivate and one that can help us navigate life's ups and downs.

There's a beautiful part of resilience that often gets overlooked and that is finding joy in the little things. Even when the world feels like it's collapsing around us, resilience helps us find joy in a good book or a hot cup of coffee. It helps us find things to be grateful for and to see the silver linings, no matter how small they might seem. Hope plays a key role in resilience, as it's not about denying the difficulties we are facing but about holding on to hope, knowing deep down that better times will come even in the darkest times. Resilience also calls for strength in the face of challenges. This strength isn't just physical; it's also emotional, psychological and spiritual. It's about digging deep within to find that inner strength to keep going, no matter how challenging the road ahead might be.

A fascinating way to observe resilience in action is by watching dogs. They live in the moment, unfazed by the past or worried about the future. They're remarkably adaptable, overcoming obstacles and hardships with grace. They love unconditionally, and they don't hold grudges. They show us a kind of resilience that's grounded in the present and buoyed by hope and love. It's as if dogs possess this inherent wisdom, an understanding that life is a mix of both, the good and the bad times, and it's all about how we navigate these times that matters. Dogs who've been abandoned, neglected or mistreated somehow maintain an amazing capacity for love and trust. Adopted into a loving family, despite their tough past, these dogs teach us a thing or two about bouncing back. They don't hang their heads in defeat; instead, they wag their tails, prance around and embrace the world with new hope and a joyful resilience that is truly amazing. Despite the trauma of their past they learn to trust and love again. They don't dwell on the past. They embrace the new opportunities that each day brings.

What could we learn from this? What if we approached life's difficulties the way dogs do? How might that change our responses, outlook and our actions when facing our own challenges? Now, I'm not saying it's easy, because it's not. It takes courage, strength and a lot of self-love to heal and move on from trauma. But, as dogs show us, it's not impossible. It's a choice we can make, to keep moving forward no matter what, and as we cultivate this resilience, just like dogs, we, too, can navigate life's storms with grace and strength. It's not the hardships that define us but how we rise above them that counts.

Isn't it fascinating to watch dogs play? They have this incredible ability to find joy in the simplest things. They could be playing with a stick they found on the ground and you'd think it was the best toy in the world by the way their tail wags. And when it rains? While we humans might complain about getting wet and the day being ruined, dogs see it as a fantastic new game, trying to catch the raindrops. They don't worry about the soggy aftermath but are just fully present, enjoying that moment. This ability to embrace the moment, no matter what it brings, is something we can learn so much from. As humans, we tend to worry too much about the future or dwell on the past, but what if we brought that dog-like spirit into our lives?

When life throws us curveballs, and it will, what if, instead of feeling overwhelmed, we looked for the stick or puddle in that situation? Maybe the stick is a hidden opportunity in a challenge or the puddle is a chance to learn and grow from a difficult situation. Imagine the freedom and happiness we could find if, like dogs, we stopped worrying about the weather and just played in the rain. After all, every storm runs out of rain eventually and, when it does, wouldn't it be amazing to look back and realise that you didn't just weather the storm, but you danced in the rain?

We have a tendency to overthink and let our worries and troubles occupy so much of our mental space that they seem bigger and scarier than they really are. Sometimes we even let these troubles define us, as if they are who we are. But have you ever seen a dog approach a hurdle? They don't stop and agonize over it or let the hurdle become their whole world. Instead, they see it as just that, a hurdle to leap over, an obstacle to conquer, not a roadblock that brings their journey to a standstill. Isn't there something incredibly inspiring about that? It's a reminder that we are not our challenges, not defined by the difficulties we face, but by how we respond to them. Our strength doesn't come from an easy journey but from the obstacles that we overcome along the way.

We've all faced moments of adversity where we've thought, *I can't get through this.* It's a natural reaction when things are tough. But what if, in those moments, we thought like a dog? Imagine it. You're facing a problem and you're feeling overwhelmed. Then you think, *What would a dog do?* Would they stop and let this hurdle define their journey or would they take a running jump, tackle it head on, and continue their journey on the other side? Chances are they'd choose the latter. Dogs don't allow setbacks to consume them. They acknowledge the hurdle, figure out a way over it and keep moving forward. They don't dwell on the setback but just focus on the path ahead. That's resilience, strength and something we can learn from.

Reflecting on resilience is one thing but expressing it is quite another, so you'll find a series of exercises at the end of this chapter designed to help you integrate the concept of resilience into your daily life. These exercises are practical activities that aim to help you understand and apply the lessons we've discussed. Do not rush through them. Approach them as you would a new friendship, with curiosity, patience and an open mind. Dogs offer us an extraordinary example of resilience, and as we learn from their approach to adversity we don't merely become better people, we become resilient individuals better equipped to handle life's ups and downs.

* * *

Exercise 1: Cultivating Optimism

The aim of this exercise is to foster a positive outlook and cultivate a mindset of gratitude, inspired by the simple joy and optimism dogs display each day. By adopting this daily habit we are encouraging our minds to focus on the good things in our lives, no matter how small, and with time and practice we will be better equipped to maintain a positive outlook in the face of difficulties and challenges.

Instructions

- Find a journal. This can be a traditional paper journal, a digital document or a dedicated app. Make it something you'll enjoy using and will have readily available.
- Choose a specific time each day for this exercise. It could be in the morning, allowing you to start your day on a positive note, or at night to reflect on the good in your day before you sleep.
- Take a few moments to think about your day and identify three things that went well or that you're grateful for. They don't have to be monumental. They could include a delicious meal, a compliment you received or a positive productive day at work.
- Jot down these three things in your journal. Try to be as specific as possible and elaborate on why they made you feel positive or grateful.
- Once you've written them down read them aloud to yourself. Hearing these positive aspects of your day reinforces their impact.

Additional Guidance

- The power of this exercise lies in its regular practice.
- If you find it difficult to identify positives or things to be grateful for don't worry. With time, this exercise can help you develop a 'positivity radar', enhancing your ability to spot these moments.
- Whenever you feel low. imagine a dog wagging its tail, ready to play or excited to see you. This mental image serves as a simple reminder of the joy and optimism we're striving to adopt.

Exercise 2: Cultivating Perseverance

We can develop perseverance and determination by tackling challenging tasks that require sustained effort, much like a dog tirelessly working at a bone. By consistently working on a challenge, we are training ourselves to persevere in the face of adversity. We're learning to approach difficulties not as impossible obstacles but as puzzles to be solved. Like a dog with a bone, never give up until you've conquered your challenge. You're stronger and more capable than you think.

Instructions

- Choose a task that you find challenging yet achievable. It could be a complex puzzle, a difficult book, a new skill or a personal goal that you've been avoiding because it seems too daunting.
- Break down the challenge into manageable parts. If it's a book decide how many pages to read each day. If it's a puzzle, allocate a specific time each day to work on it. A large task becomes less overwhelming when tackled bit by bit.
- Dedicate a specific time each day to work on your chosen challenge. Consistency is key in developing perseverance.
- Keep a log of your progress. Celebrate small victories, like completing a chapter of the book or a part of the puzzle. This will motivate you to keep going.
- There may be days when you feel like giving up. Don't. Remember, the aim of this exercise is to build perseverance. Think of the dog with the bone. No matter how hard the bone seems, the dog doesn't give up.

Additional Guidance

- Remember that perseverance is about endurance and consistent effort. Don't rush through the task. Take your time.
- Don't be disheartened by mistakes or setbacks. They are a part of the process. Learn from them and keep moving forward.
- Maintain a positive attitude. Celebrate your progress no matter how small it may seem.
- Just like a dog visualises getting to the marrow of the bone, visualise your success. This will keep you motivated.
- If you're feeling overwhelmed ask for help or seek advice. You're not in this alone.

Exercise 3: Embracing Change

We have the capacity to adapt, grow and thrive in the face of change. By practicing the art of adaptability, we're developing a valuable skill that not only enhances our resilience but also opens up new possibilities and experiences in life.

Instructions

- Begin by selecting one small change you can make to your daily routine. This could be taking a new route to work, trying a different type of cuisine or changing up your morning routine.
- Once you've decided on the change, spend some time planning how you will implement it. For example, if you've chosen a new route to work map it out beforehand.
- Now it's time to embrace the change. Put your plan into action. Drive the new route to work, order from that new restaurant you've never tried or wake up fifteen minutes earlier to meditate.
- Reflect on how it felt to implement this change. Was it uncomfortable, exciting or a bit of both? Write your thoughts and feelings in a journal.
- Once you feel comfortable with one change introduce another. The goal is to become more adaptable and comfortable with change.

Additional Guidance

- The changes you choose should be small at first. The aim isn't to overhaul your life overnight but gradually become more comfortable with change.
- It may feel uncomfortable at first, and that's okay. Remember, it's natural to feel resistance to change. Be patient with yourself.
- Don't forget to acknowledge and celebrate your willingness to embrace change. Each step, no matter how small, is progress.
- Frame the change in a positive light. Rather than thinking of it as an inconvenience, consider it a new adventure, or an

opportunity to learn.

- When faced with change, dogs don't dwell on what they're leaving behind. They explore their new environment with curiosity and excitement. Try to adopt this mindset as you navigate through your changes.

* * *

CHAPTER 11: INTUITION

Eating chips covered with a lashing of salt and vinegar at the seaside. That is a must-do activity as often as time and opportunity allow. It had been worth standing in the queue for twenty minutes to buy my chips however, I didn't realise at the time that a beady pair of eyes were watching my every move. Freshly cooked and perfectly delicious I justified the calories by knowing that I had planned to go on a long walk on the beach whilst eating them. The best exercise.

I had only been on the beach long enough to eat two chips when a man walking past in the opposite direction lunged and grabbed my arm, pulling me towards him. Startled, I attempted to pull away, my heart hammering in my chest. Was this some sort of attack? He covered my chips with his hand and used his other arm to make a wild circle in the air above my head.

'There you go.' He grinned.

'I just saved your chips from a furious looking seagull. You were about to be dive-bombed and robbed! Hope you get to enjoy them now.'

I looked over as the seagull swooped away in his hunt for a less well-defended lunch. As the man ambled away along the beach, I contemplated the kindness of strangers. I thought of how my first instinct was one of attack and mistrust. Maybe I needed to rethink how I read my intuition. It's good to know that there is always someone who will save the days of being able to eat chips in peace on the beach. These are to be preserved at all costs.

Are you familiar with that sensation in your stomach that gently nudges you in a direction, almost like a subtle whisper, saying, 'Hey, this way.' We all have it, but the question is, how often do we really listen to it? That gentle nudge, the faint whisper that suggests a certain path, that's our intuition. It's something we all possess, but how often do we really pay attention to it? We get so caught up in our thoughts, plans and our worries that we often drown out that little voice and fail to hear it.

Take a moment and think about dogs. It's incredible, isn't it, how they seem to know things before they happen? They'll be calmly lying down, and then suddenly, their ears perk up, tail starts wagging and they're at the door just as the doorbell rings. Dogs seem to have an internal radar, but it's just their intuition, their sixth sense, that's working its magic. We humans have a similar system too; it's just that we seldom listen to it or know what it is.

Our intuition is like this inner compass, guiding us, giving us nudges and whispers. It's an internal system that's always working, trying to help us navigate our true path. But how often do we listen to it? How often do we trust it? We've learned to rely heavily on logic and reason, which certainly have their place, but our intuition can offer a different kind of wisdom, one that is more holistic and often more in tune with our deepest needs and desires. The next time you get that feeling in your gut, that gentle nudge saying 'Hey, this way', pay attention, listen to it and trust it, because just like a dog trusts its intuition to sense what's coming, we can trust our intuition to guide us on our path. It's a part of us, just waiting to be heard, waiting to be trusted. And who knows, it might just lead us exactly where we need to go.

Trusting that inner voice can be a difficult at first. Our minds are often buzzing with thoughts, worries and to-do lists. Amidst all of the noise it can be difficult to notice that quiet whisper of our intuition. But then again, look at how our dogs live their lives. They don't sit around overthinking or complicating things. They're guided by their instincts, responding to the world in a way that's incredibly intuitive. They live in the present, making the most of each moment, and they're exceptionally good at tuning in to their inner guidance system.

Dogs' instincts are deeply ingrained behaviours that have been passed down from their wild ancestors, fine-tuned by nature over thousands of years. They have acute senses and a superior sense of smell and hearing compared to us, allowing them to pick up on subtle cues in their environment. It's not uncommon for dogs to react to something we humans are blissfully unaware of, like an imminent storm, an intruder or even changes in our health. This is their survival instinct in action, honed by their ancestors who relied on these senses for hunting, protection and general survival in the wild. Another fascinating area is their social instincts. Have you ever noticed your dog watching you intently while you're busy in the kitchen or while you're glued to your laptop screen? Dogs are social animals, and this instinctive behaviour allows them to understand and respond to the actions of their pack, and in this case, you and your family. This instinct allows dogs to form deep bonds with their human families and communicate effectively.

How do we identify this voice of intuition amidst the noise in our minds? Intuition often comes as a feeling or a sense rather than a thought. It might be a gut feeling, a sudden sense of clarity, a wave of peace or an unexplained sense of unease or caution about a particular situation. Learning to identify and trust our intuition involves becoming more attuned to these subtle signals from our bodies and minds. This requires practicing mindfulness, quieting our thoughts and really listening to what our inner self is trying to tell us. It might not always make logical sense, and that's okay. Intuition is not always about logic but about a deeper, more instinctual understanding. If we live more in the moment, like dogs do, we might find it easier to tune into our intuition. By stepping back from our constant worries and to-do lists and instead place our focus on the present, we allow space for our intuition to come through.

Intuition springs up spontaneously; it's a sudden 'knowing', much like a dog's alertness to a distant sound way before our human ears catch it. Can you recall a similar sudden instinct or 'knowing' that popped up within you? That's intuition. It often nudges us towards actions that contribute to a broader good, beyond just our personal gains. It's as if it's woven into the tapestry of a bigger picture, subtly aligning us with the greater harmony of life. Unlike our ever-changing thoughts that can scatter in any direction, our intuition remains steady. It's a constant companion offering us reliable and unchanging inner truths. Have you felt this steadfast voice within you? That's your intuition, communicating in its consistent comforting tone.

So, how can we strengthen our intuitive muscle, make this voice louder and clearer? The answer lies in something as profound as it is simple: gratitude. It has the power to transform our perception and allows us to see things as they truly are, free of fear or selfish desires. In this state of grace, we are better able to spot intuitive nudges guiding us towards our highest good. With this in mind, I invite you to a challenge. The next time you feel a subtle stir within, a thought or a feeling that seems to stand out, pause. Take a breath. Acknowledge it. Trust it. Engage in a conversation with yourself, asking, 'Could this be my intuition guiding me?' Then, be still and see where this dialogue leads.

So, why should we trust our intuition? One of the main reasons is because it's usually grounded in your subconscious mind, which is constantly gathering and analysing information, even when you're not consciously aware of it. Your intuition is like your brain's way of cutting through the clutter and giving you the crucial information you need to make a decision. This means that often your intuition is not just a random feeling but a conclusion drawn from a vast amount of information processed at a subconscious level. It plays a valuable role in decision-making, especially when we face complex situations that logic and reason may not navigate. In such cases, our intuition can guide us towards choices that align with our deepest values and personal truths. When you get a gut feeling about something it's your brain trying to tell you that there's more to the situation than meets the eye. Let's consider a real-life scenario. Say you meet someone for the first time and instantly you feel uneasy even though, on the surface, everything seems fine. This could be your intuition alerting you to subtle cues that your conscious mind has not yet processed.

Trusting our intuition encourages us to trust ourselves. It's about honouring our feelings and our individual experiences. When we listen to our intuition we validate our ability to look inward for answers and affirm our capacity to understand and interpret our personal experiences. In a way, trusting our intuition is an act of self-trust and self-belief. It's a declaration that says, 'I trust my feelings. I trust my experiences. I trust myself.' Not that we should toss logic out the window. It's about balancing our rational thinking and our intuitive understanding. It's about using all the tools at our disposal, those of logic, reason and intuition to navigate the journey of life. So, what is your intuition trying to tell you? Take a moment and listen. What is it saying? Can it be guiding you towards something important? Remember, your intuition is a powerful ally, so don't be afraid to trust it.

We have learnt how dogs trust their instincts without question. They react to the world in instinctive, intuitive ways, and we can learn from their example. By embracing the qualities of intuition, its spontaneity, guidance towards the greater good and constant presence, we can learn to trust this internal compass in our own lives. Trusting our intuition is ultimately an act of self-trust, an affirmation saying, 'I trust myself.' With this newfound understanding of intuition, I encourage you to engage with the exercises following this chapter. They're designed to help you develop your intuitive abilities. By practicing these exercises you'll deepen your understanding and further integrate this learning into your daily life. Trust the process, trust your intuition and see where it leads you. Who knows what you might discover?

* * *

Exercise 1: Flex Your Intuition Muscle

The aim of this exercise is to cultivate trust in your intuition by making small, everyday decisions, based solely on your gut feelings. Over time, this exercise will help you form a stronger connection with your intuition. You'll learn to trust that internal voice guiding you, just as a dog instinctively trusts its senses. As you grow more comfortable with small decisions, you can start applying this trust to bigger decisions, enhancing your overall ability to navigate life intuitively.

Instructions

- Choose small non-critical decisions in your everyday life where you can practice using your intuition. This could be choosing what to eat for lunch, deciding which book to read next or taking a different route to work or home.
- Close your eyes and take a deep breath. Tune in to your body and ask yourself what you genuinely want or feel drawn towards. For example, if you're deciding on a book, try holding each option in your hand and see which one resonates with you.

- Decide based solely on your gut feeling without over analysing or overthinking. The idea here is to trust your intuition, so go with what you feel.
- Follow through with your decision. Eat the lunch you chose, start reading the book or drive along the new route.
- After you've followed through, reflect on the outcome. How did the decision turn out? Did you enjoy the meal, the book or the drive? Did something unexpected or positive happen because of this decision?

Additional Guidance

- Be patient with yourself. Trusting your intuition is a skill that develops over time.
- Remember, there are no 'wrong' outcomes in this exercise. Even if a decision didn't turn out as expected, it's still a valuable lesson in understanding and trusting your intuition.
- Try to do this exercise regularly. The more you practice the more you'll start to recognise and trust your intuitive impulses.
- Keep a journal of these exercises. Write what you felt and the outcomes. You'll start seeing patterns that will help you understand how your intuition speaks to you.

Exercise 2: Body Scan. Tuning in to Your Inner Wisdom

The aim of this exercise is to cultivate an awareness of the physical sensations in your body to tap into your intuitive wisdom. Our bodies often hold and communicate intuitive messages, which can manifest as physical sensations, like a knot in our stomach or a flutter in our chest. Over time, regular body scans can help you become more in tune with your body's wisdom and strengthen your relationship with your intuition. You will instinctively know when something's amiss, you'll start to recognise and trust your body's intuitive signals.

Instructions

- Find a quiet, comfortable place where you can relax without being disturbed.
- You can either lie down, sit or recline. Just ensure you're in a position that allows you to relax and pay attention to your body without straining.
- Close your eyes and take a few deep breaths, inhaling deeply through your nose and exhaling through your mouth.
- Starting from the top of your head, slowly scan down through your body, paying attention to each part as you go. Notice any sensations you feel in each area.
- Pay particular attention to any areas that feel tense, heavy or uncomfortable. There might be a knot in your stomach, a tightness in your chest or tension in your shoulders. Try not to judge or change these sensations. Just acknowledge them as they are.
- If you feel a significant sensation, ask yourself if there's any intuitive message associated with it. For example, if you notice a knot in your stomach ask yourself, 'What is my intuition trying to tell me?'
- Listen to any thoughts, feelings or images that come up. Intuition often speaks subtly and symbolically.

Additional Guidance

- This exercise is about observation not interpretation. Don't worry if you don't receive clear intuitive messages immediately. The aim is to become more aware of your body and the sensations within it.
- Practice this exercise regularly. The more you do it the better you'll become at noticing and interpreting your body's intuitive signals.
- If you're having trouble tuning into your body, you might find

guided body scan meditations helpful, at least in the beginning.

- Keep a journal of your body scan experiences. Write about any sensations you felt and the insights that arose. Over time, you'll see patterns and gain a deeper understanding of how your intuition communicates with you.

Exercise 3: Dream Analysis. Decoding Your Subconscious

This exercise connects with your subconscious mind through your dreams. By keeping a dream journal and analysing recurring themes or symbols, you may uncover messages from your intuition. Dreams are a powerful medium through which your subconscious communicates with you. Just like dogs, your subconscious and intuition communicate in their unique language. By learning this language through your dreams, you can strengthen your relationship with your intuition and trust it more in your daily life.

Instructions

- Keep a journal and pen by your bed. It's important to record your dreams as soon as you wake up, as they can quickly fade from memory.
- Upon waking, before you get out of bed or fully awaken, write about your dreams in as much detail as possible. Record the events, characters, emotions and specific symbols or themes that stood out.
- Look for patterns in your dreams over time. Are there recurring symbols, themes or scenarios? Do certain emotions tend to surface in your dreams?
- Analyse your dreams in the context of your life. What might the recurring symbols or themes represent? Is there a connection to current situations or feelings in your waking life?

Additional Guidance

- Do not censor or judge your dreams. Even if they seem strange or irrational record everything you remember.
- Consider using a dream dictionary or resource to help you understand common symbols and themes in dreams, but remember, the meanings are not one-size-fits-all. Your personal context and feelings about the symbols are crucial.
- Be patient with this process. It may take some time before clear patterns or messages emerge. The important thing is to maintain the habit of recording and reflecting on your dreams.
- Not every dream holds a profound intuitive message. Some dreams may be influenced by daily events, anxieties or your physical state.

* * *

CONCLUSION

As we come to the end of our journey looking into the extraordinary traits of dogs and the lessons they offer us, we can see the huge opportunity for personal growth and happiness they offer. Dogs are more than best friends; they're emotional superheroes. They approach each day with boundless joy, unshakeable loyalty and a love that is both deep and unconditional. They show us that love, in its purest form, is the most precious gift we can offer to the world and ourselves, a gift that floods our lives with warmth, kindness and affection.

Imagine channelling the same level of loyalty showed by our dogs into our human relationships. Picture friendships reflecting the constancy and faithfulness of a dog, friends who affirm your worth, particularly on the days you doubt yourself. Dogs also teach us about the power of forgiveness. They live in the moment, holding no grudges, showing us that forgiveness isn't a grand gesture but a life-altering choice. By letting go of past wounds we can unburden ourselves, moving towards a lighter happier state of being.

Dogs guide us in expressing our needs and understanding of non-verbal cues, which can enhance our relationships, so why not voice your needs more assertively? They also remind us of the power of gentle touch and loving glances. They teach us empathy, mindfulness, self-care and the necessity of play. While these may seem like simple lessons, their conscious use can bring about a meaningful change in our lives.

Through dogs we learn that aging comes with its own beauty, dignity and wisdom. They teach us about aging gracefully, showing us it's not just about aches or greying hair but resilience, understanding our bodies and adapting to changes, knowing that age is just a number and it's our spirit that can stay forever youthful and playful. As we embrace these lessons, we might find ourselves less fearful of aging and more prepared to embrace the joy and wisdom each day brings. We can be inspired to tackle challenges with resilience, viewing setbacks as hurdles, not roadblocks. The next time you face adversity ask yourself, what would a dog do? This dog-inspired resilience can be nurtured through practical exercises included in this book. These activities aim to help you understand and embody resilience, transforming you into someone better equipped to handle life's highs and lows. As our journey together through the lessons comes to an end, let us remember the lesson of mindfulness. It's not merely a concept; it's a way of life, effortlessly exemplified by dogs. Through mindfulness, we hear and notice the things in life that are often overlooked, such as that small nudge of intuition, guiding us towards our higher good.

Reflect on which chapter resonated with you the most. How can you implement its exercises to develop the trait you wish to expand? These exercises are designed to help you gradually integrate these teachings into your life. They form a toolkit for living a dog-inspired life. Use them to understand yourself better, practice forgiveness more readily, communicate more effectively, relish the small joys, care for yourself better and bring a dose of playful spirit into your everyday life.

Remember, improving our lives isn't a one-off task but an ongoing process. We're continuously learning and growing. It's never too late to start this journey, which can be a joyful, positive and hopeful adventure. As this book concludes, I share your excitement as you embark on your new journey. Remember, you're not alone. We're all on this path together, continually learning, developing, and uncovering the authentic aspects of our true selves. It's your turn to apply the profound wisdom from this book into your life. You're equipped with knowledge, insights, and readiness for this journey of self-discovery and growth. Embrace it confidently, knowing that you're prepared, ready and that you're going to do great.

❋ ❋ ❋

ADDITIONAL INFORMATION

Thank you for choosing to read this book and I hope the knowledge you've gained has enhanced many aspects of your life.

If you have a keen interest in learning and want to explore how dogs can be your ultimate life coach take a look at our online courses.

https://payhip.com/animalhealingtherapy

Loving the Journey: The Dog Inspired Guide to Lasting Weight Loss and Well-Being

For keen learners this online course expands the teachings found in The Dog Life Coach book series. It uncovers more secrets to successful weight loss and well-being through practical tools and tailored insights.

On the course you will learn how to view setbacks as stepping stones and swap fear for love, just as dogs naturally do; it's a transformative journey toward self-love as the ultimate healer.

The course will enable you to fully understand the emotional toll of weight fluctuations and self-doubt – experiences shared by many. You will explores the psychological impact associated with weight loss efforts, with guidance on building resilience, boosting self-esteem and prioritising holistic well-being.

If you're tired of regaining weight and long for a new approach to lasting weight loss and well-being this course is for you. Change your relationship with your body, break free from industry norms and become the best version of yourself. Enrol and let the journey to lasting well-being begin.

The Wisdom Within: Embracing Life's Lesson's Through Dogs

In this course you'll explore the remarkable qualities of dogs, such as loyalty, presence and intuition, applying their life lessons to enhance your well-being. Through practical exercises in intuition, mindfulness and animal communication, you'll develop emotional awareness, refine communication skills and achieve a newfound sense of balance, inner peace and fulfilment.

* * *

To continue your discovery to a more fulfilling and joyful life check out the following titles in The Dog Life Coach book series:

Mastering Confidence. Lessons from the Dog Life Coach.

The Dog Life Coach's Guide to Weight Loss and Well-Being

* * *

Take the next step and join us in The Dog Life Coach Club.

https://subscribepage.io/TheClub

For exclusive updates, bonus content and the chance to connect with others on a similar journey, we encourage you to sign up for our newsletter.

Joining The Dog Life Coach Club grants you access to regular insights, special offers, and a supportive community that shares a passion for dogs and the pursuit of a more fulfilling life. Here's to celebrating the lessons of loyalty, resilience, and love, and to living each day with the spirit of being more dog!

* * *

BOOKS BY THIS AUTHOR

Mastering Confidence: Lessons From The Dog Life Coach

Do you ever find yourself in moments of self-doubt, questioning your own abilities, wishing for more self-confidence?

Do you find it difficult to trust again because of past hurt and betrayal, resulting in a loss of confidence in your own judgment?

Are you trapped in life's constant rush, losing confidence and struggling to stay present or find your true purpose?

Are you tired of feeling like an imposter in your own life and career?

Mastering Confidence: Lessons from The Dog Life Coach is your ticket to unshakable confidence. Within these pages you'll find practical exercises that can help you unlock your full potential.

Step into a world where trust, purpose, and rock-solid confidence are your companions. Leave self-doubt and anxiety behind as you embrace self-acceptance, resilience, and empowerment. Learn to be as authentic, compassionate, and empathetic as the dogs who inspire us. Find forgiveness, loyalty, and presence in every moment.

It's time to embrace the incredible qualities dogs offer and discover a more confident and fulfilling life. Open the pages of this book and let your dog be your guide to a life brimming with authenticity and happiness.

Welcome the journey, accept who you are, and enjoy newfound confidence.

The Dog Life Coach's Guide To Weight Loss And Well-Being

Are you tired of the endless cycle of dieting and weight gain?

Do you struggle with self-doubt and low self-esteem because of your weight?

Are you frustrated with the one-size-fits-all approach of the weight loss industry?

Worried about the health implications of your weight and not sure where to start?

Do you find it challenging to maintain motivation and stay on track?

Join the wonderful world of dogs and uncover essential qualities that can lead you to a healthier, happier self. Dogs teach us about loyalty, resilience, empathy, adaptability and living life to the fullest. By embracing these qualities and adding in some self-care and mindfulness, you'll find your way to lasting well-being and successful weight loss.

This journey is about more than just shedding pounds; it's about embracing self-love as the ultimate healer and unlocking a vibrant, healthy, and happy version of yourself. We'll show you how to swap fear for love, just like dogs do, and view setbacks as stepping stones to your goals.

The emotional toll of weight fluctuations, self-doubt, and the overwhelming influence of the weight loss industry is a shared experience. This book takes a look at the psychological impact of weight fluctuations on self-esteem and overall well-being, offering valuable guidance on building resilience, boosting self-esteem, and prioritising holistic well-being.

The 'Dog Life Coach's Guide to Weight Loss and Well-Being' isn't your typical weight loss book. It's a holistic approach to managing life's ups and downs, facing challenges and discovering your true self. If you're tired of the weight loss rollercoaster, this book is your partner on the journey to becoming a healthier, happier you.

Printed in Great Britain
by Amazon

39856696R00086